GOING TO MULLINIX
Mostly Gentle Tales
About Mostly Gentle Folks
and Curious Critters

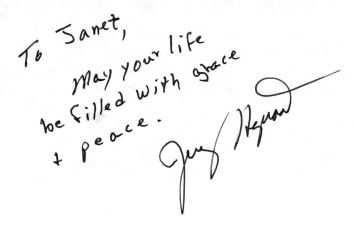

To Janet,
May your life
be filled with grace
+ peace.

Jerry Haywood

JERRY HAYWOOD

© 2018

Published in the United States by Nurturing Faith Inc., Macon GA,

www.nurturingfaith.net.

Library of Congress Cataloging-in-Publication Data is available.

ISBN 978-1-63528-030-2

Contents

Prologue: Going to Mullinix v

Part One: In the Beginning
I Am a Victim... 2
Grace Lessons at a Livestock Auction....................................... 5
No Crying in a Ford Pickup 8
Simple Shopping 11
The Right Time 14
A Muddy Baptism 19
In the Heart of a Child 25
The Last Corn-shucking 29

Part Two: Intriguing Characters
Grand Canyon Cowboy... 34
Redneck Angel on Interstate 95 37
Smelling Like Easter 40
A Good Day?.. 43
Daffodils and Discipleship 46
Is God Ever Too Busy? 48
The Master or the Masters? 51
Robbing Us of Our "Insanity" 55
Seven Miles from Home 58

Part Three: Curious Critters
Bully Fish Need Love Too... 62
Ducks Don't Notice the Unexpected.. 64
Looking Back with Hands on the Plow.................................... 68
Does Jesus Care about Harelip Puppies? 72
The Many Sides of a Canada Goose.. 75
Eagles Eat Roadkill Too 79
Locked In with Our Fears 82
Standing with the Goats 85

Part Four: Family Life

From Playhouse to Horror House to Playhouse 90

Waiting for the Boil 93

A Small Man? 96

A Bloody Thanksgiving.. 100

I Want You Where I Can See You 103

A Persistent Light 105

River Journeying.. 107

Too Old to Eat Cornbread... 110

A Father's Love and Healing Scars... 114

A Garden of Gratitude 117

A Last Christmas 120

Part Five: Church Life

Foolishness in Need of Grace 126

Living Each Day to the Fullest... 129

Overexpecting? 132

Attacked in a Grocery Store 135

Shotgun Christians 139

A Wedding Tornado 144

"I'm Going to See Jesus" 149

Part Six: Health Issues

The Dangers of Doctor Visits.. 154

Vicarious Eating 157

Bright Lights and Inside Doctors 160

Part Seven: Passing Thoughts

How I Got Jimmy Carter Elected President............................. 166

Don't Judge My Fear of Flying.. 170

Too Small? 173

At a Bar in Key West... 176

Good Stories Never Grow Old... 179

Epilogue: Coming Home 183

Prologue: Going to Mullinix

It was a familiar question in that close-knit rural community of Chip, North Carolina: "Where're you going, Arthur?" In reality it was more of a greeting than a nosy inquiry, but my Pa-Pa's answer was always the same. "Going to Mullinix," he would call out cheerfully.

My maternal grandfather and I traveled to many places in his dark green Ford pickup, but we never made it to Mullinix. In fact, we were never quite sure where it was, or maybe we were a little fearful that if we made it all the way, our journey would be over. Pa-Pa did so enjoy the journey.

I rode with Pa-Pa (with an emphasis on each syllable; not Papa, the name my grandchildren have given me), to deliver chicken feed around the Chip community, halfway between Mt. Gilead and Troy in the Piedmont region of North Carolina. We also made once-a-week trips to Hamlet and Rockingham to deliver eggs and chickens. But in truth we were always on the way to Mullinix.

I vividly remember the day I asked Pa-Pa where Mullinix was located and if he had ever been there. He chuckled and reflected for a moment before answering: "No, son. I've never been there. But I've seen the sign."

"Where?" I persisted. I was usually a little too shy to be this insistent with adults, but I figured if we were always "going to Mullinix," I'd like to know more about it.

"Cain't rightly recall where I saw it," Pa-Pa replied vaguely. "Few years back. But I 'member what it looked like."

He was quiet again, so I assumed that was the end of the conversation, although my curiosity was far from satisfied. But after a few more minutes of silence, Pa-Pa resumed his story of Mullinix with a faraway look in his eyes as if he were recalling the details of a fading memory.

"It was an old, scaling, wooden, black-and-white sign with the letters growing dim, but I could still read it," Pa-Pa said, much quieter than usual. "M-u-l-l-i-n-i-x. Mullinix."

"But you never followed the sign?" I asked, surprised at the courage of my persistence. Pa-Pa usually did most of the talking.

His eyes got that distant look again as he continued, "Couldn't rightly tell which way it was a-pointin'. The pointing piece of board on top was loose and almost falling off, and the post in the ground holding the top board was all twisted." Shaking his head, Pa-Pa repeated, "Couldn't rightly tell which way it was a-pointin'. Not even sure whether it was a place or the name of the road."

But just recalling the name again sent Pa-Pa into his unique laughter. Pa-Pa had the ability to find humor in most things, and we usually laughed at the same things, but I failed to find the humor in "Mullinix." It sounded like a reasonable name to me. I even liked the way it rolled off my tongue and tickled the roof of my mouth.

Maybe Pa-Pa found the name more enjoyable than humorous too, because for whatever reason, he was always "going to Mullinix." Even when he would step out of the sitting room at his home to draw a bucket of water from the well just outside the back screen porch door and his family would ask where he was going, Pa-Pa would reply, "Going to Mullinix."

I guess I've also been "going to Mullinix" most of my life.

When I was very young, with a child's overblown sensitivity to a frightening world, Mullinix became a place in my imagination where I could go when things became too harsh or too frightening or too hopeless. In my little boy's mind Mullinix was that magical place where all the scattered pieces of life fit together and dreams came true and hopes were realized and empty places were filled.

When I became a man and later a pastor, Mullinix became for me a symbol for that place where God's kingdom has come fully "on earth as it is in heaven" (Matt 6:10). Somewhere along the way, I began remembering those early years, and Mullinix became for me the closest we can come to "home" in this world while our citizenship papers are in another world.

I realize that I will never make it all the way, just as my Pa-Pa and I never made it all the way to Mullinix in his Ford pickup. Totally becoming the creatures we were meant to be is not possible in this world. In fact, much of the time I find myself so far from the goal that my destination appears hidden, as if surrounded by a dense fog, and I can only trust that it is still somewhere up ahead.

The journey toward that unattainable place, however, is what gives my life meaning, joy, and direction. The effort to "be conformed to the image of his Son" (Rom 8:29) contains at least the potential of my being "reclaimed by the Christ" at a level I had never thought possible.

Simply put, "going to Mullinix" became for me something of a metaphor for the walk of discipleship in which I learn kingdom lessons from the constant companionship of the risen Lord and am gradually transformed into his image by generous portions of unfathomable grace.

I suppose, in a sense, that means the destination and the journey are all of one piece. I walk in that level of kingdom living I have already attained while at the same time reaching for a higher plane.

On my best days I have tried to invite the Christ into all the areas of my life as a constant controlling companion. On the days when I am not at my best, I have been gifted with "signs" in the form of people, critters, and events that have pointed me back toward the Way. This book tells the stories of just a few of those people, critters, and events.

My constant challenge has been to notice when I encounter the signs, when God appears in plain sight in the most ordinary of places. Often, the sign provides just a hint of the sacred. At other times, the sign comes as a firm nudge down a path still fresh with God's footprints.

So, like I said, I must remain awake and alert each day and each moment or I am in danger of losing my way.

I don't know how successful I will be in my journey toward modeling the Christ, standing for that which he stood for, living and dying as he lived and died. But I believe faith requires that I begin and continue in the spirit of the apostle Paul, who wrote to those Philippians struggling to find their way in this new faith: "Not that I have already obtained all this, or have already been made perfect, but I press on to take hold of that for which Christ Jesus took hold of me" (Phil 3:12).

Besides, if I'm not "going to Mullinix," where am I going?

Part One

In the Beginning

I Am a Victim

"Just relax and work it out," my tech-savvy wife, Jean, says calmly, wondering why I teeter on the edge of a moderate to severe panic attack when anything technological goes slightly askew.

She does not understand. I am a victim of my childhood, which has afflicted me with a severe case of TAI (technology anger issues).

The childhood I'm speaking of is that period between approximately nine and 12 years of age when I rode with my grandfather, Pa-Pa, in his green Ford pickup around the little rural community of Chip.

Pa-Pa did not trust any motorized vehicles except Fords. "Only thing on the road you can count on," he would argue. He was a stubborn man and a sometimes irreverent teaser who didn't mind arguing about most anything, mostly just for the fun of it, because Pa-Pa loved to laugh.

I enjoyed hearing his laughter and joining in, except for those times when it was directed at me. But that's another story.

Pa-Pa's laugh began as a deep, throaty chuckle that quickly accelerated into laughter too deep for sound as his face reddened with the suppressed strain of it all. Following that brief silence of internal jollity, the laugh finally exploded into a powerful expiration of trapped air, concluding with a gasp and the exclamation, "Ahhh, law." The final stage of laughter involved a slow side-to-side shaking of his large head as he wiped his eyes and red-veined long face with his ever-present white handkerchief.

As I said, I rode with Pa-Pa to deliver chicken feed to neighboring farmers and on his once-a-week trips to Hamlet and Rockingham, where he had a market for his chickens and eggs.

The way I understood it, Pa-Pa would construct the chicken house and provide the brood biddies and the feed, and the farmers would contribute the labor until the chickens were full-grown, able to produce eggs or fill cooking pots for Sunday dinners.

The headquarters of this business was housed in Pa-Pa's country store across the road from the family home. On rare days when Pa-Pa and Lon Eury, the graying, overalls-wearing store clerk, would be away on the same day, Pa-Pa entrusted me with minding the little country store. I was pleased with his faith in a 10-year-old boy.

My brief sense of importance was quickly smothered, however, under the fear of the ancient manually operated cash register that rested on the counter behind the open boxes of two-for-a-penny candy.

Pa-Pa had carefully explained the proper way to make entries on the long, upward curved keys and then record them by pulling the large metal handle on the right side of the huge cash register toward the countertop until the drawer popped out. But somehow I missed the lesson on how to delete an entry and start over. I quickly discovered that, for me, that was the most important lesson of all.

Often, I had to make an entry three or four times before I got it right. And the more times I entered the wrong amount, the more panicky I would become as my trembling fingers almost involuntarily hit incorrect key after incorrect key.

Late that afternoon, I would watch anxiously as Pa-Pa checked the day's cash register tape with a frown, wondering how I sold items for $.05, $.55, $5.50, and $55.00 all in a row. I was deeply grateful when, in his kindness, Pa-Pa refused to humiliate me by calling attention to my mistakes, although it was obvious he never got the money in the cash drawer to match my erratic entries on the tape.

On the silent, still nights following my mismanagement of the store, I would have nightmares of huge monsters taking the shape of gigantic cash registers with metal handles for legs, upward curved register keys for teeth, and a large cash-drawer mouth that threatened to delete me with one rapid gulp.

Undoubtedly, my wife should understand that my aversion to all things technological is the result of victimization. It isn't my fault; my Pa-Pa should never have left me in charge of that store. So don't make me feel guilty when, with trembling hands, I hold out my iPhone, laptop, or tablet, frantically asking, "Could you fix this?" I confess that most of time I forget to say "please."

Every once in a while, I wonder if that's what the journey to Mullinix is all about: discovering the strength to change; allowing the power of God's kingdom to take over me so I am not a prisoner of my past but have a future filled with newness and unrealized potential. Maybe being a citizen of the kingdom of heaven means, in part, that I can cease being a victim.

That thought particularly enters my mind when my wife hands my corrected iPhone back to me with the not-so-subtle hint that I need to grow up. At such times I wonder if Jean has come across these words in her nightly devotional readings: "God has not given us the spirit of fear, but of power, and of love, and of a sound mind" (2 Tim 1:7).

Well, I don't have nightmares of cash-register monsters anymore, and yesterday I tried to unravel a problem with my laptop all by myself with only a hint of anger and a barely discernible increase in my heart rate.

That may mean I'm getting closer to Mullinix and the goal of winning "the prize for which God has called me heavenward in Christ Jesus" (Phil 3:14).

Grace Lessons at a Livestock Auction

As much as I enjoyed hearing my Pa-Pa's big laugh, it was no fun at all when it was directed at me. Thankfully, that happened only rarely, but when it did, it was intense and often humiliating.

I went to a livestock auction with my Pa-Pa and Uncle G. A., my mother's only surviving brother, once, and once was enough. It was a cruel circus of animals of all kinds and sizes brought in by farmers hoping for top dollar from the meat processors bidding for the choice pieces of meat. Very quickly I discovered that to the auction personnel, that's all these animals were. Humane treatment was unnecessary since even small calves, left tethered and waterless in the scorching heat all day, were only pieces of meat.

That was a traumatic experience for a young boy of 10 who had always regarded farm animals as companions and friends. Inside the pens of the auction house, even the harmless smaller animals were poked and pummeled and pulled mercilessly with shepherd crooks for no apparent reason except to satisfy the sadistic streaks of the auction personnel.

In one corner pen I was horrified to see a man standing on the top boards of a sturdy pen containing a huge bull. The man held a long leather strap that descended again and again on the back, head, nose, legs, and other body parts of the bull, which desperately thrashed around in that small enclosure, seeking a way out of his torment. That experience no doubt accounts for the fact that even today when I catch a glimpse of a bullfight or the running of the bulls on ESPN, I instinctively pull for the bulls. I know that doesn't sound very Christian, but, like I said, that auction experience at a young age had a profound lasting effect on me.

Turning my back on the sounds and sights of the needless cruelty, I walked quickly out of the pen area to find my Pa-Pa. I located him silently watching a tethered calf with sunken sides and dry tongue hanging low, breathing hard. Shaking his head and clucking his tongue, he said, "They're too rough on these animals." I felt very close to him in that moment.

That warm feeling did not last long, however. Wandering from trailer to trailer, most pulled by pickups displeasing to my Pa-Pa because they were not all Fords,

I casually looked through the slats at the various animals that had not yet been unloaded. Most were standing casually, oblivious to their approaching fate.

I paused at one long farm trailer hauling a milk cow and noticed that she had a serious intestinal problem. The rear slats of the trailer gate were dripping with slimy, wet cow feces. Automatically, I took a couple steps back so as not to accidentally get any of the filth on my clean shirt and jeans.

I didn't step back far enough.

A man standing to my right casually reached through the slats and squeezed the filthy tail of the cow. A sound like a rifle shot reverberated in my ears as I was suddenly blinded by cow dung. Laughter exploded around me as the man with the curious hand justified himself by muttering, "I just wanted to see if her tail was soft."

The cow obviously did not want anyone messing with her tail and had violently kicked the dripping gate, spraying filth in all directions but mostly toward me as I was in direct line with the back end of the cow.

My world was suddenly transformed into a black-and-white polka dot pattern. Horrified, I realized that my eyeballs must have been partially covered with smatterings of cow dung. Disoriented and confused, I stumbled around looking for my uncle and Pa-Pa. Surely they would give me the sympathy I desperately needed, surrounded as I was by raucous laughter.

I should have known better. My uncle liked to laugh as much as my Pa-Pa, which is understandable since he was, after all, George Arthur Haywood Jr., a chip off the old block, especially when it came to finding humor in most everything. The humor in this catastrophe was evidently not difficult to find.

Blind as I was, it didn't take me long to find them since I heard Pa-Pa begin the first stage of his big laugh on the edge of the bobbing, laughing crowd. As I approached, Pa-Pa walked off to continue the next phases of his patented laugh without my suffering the further humiliation of having to listen to him. He didn't walk off far enough because I heard him wheezing in the distance, even as I became aware of my Uncle G. A. standing before me, taking out his handkerchief in a hand trembling from the strain of suppressed hilarity.

Uncle G. A.'s attempt to suppress his laughter was only slightly successful as we found an outdoor spigot under which he soaked his handkerchief and began the hopeless task of wiping the hundreds of spots of cow dung off my face and clothes. He did the best he could, but it's difficult to do a good job at anything when you're bent over at the waist with uncontrollable laughter.

Going to Mullinix

For the next half hour it was wipe and laugh, wipe and laugh, wipe and laugh.

"Son," Uncle G. A. finally gasped, "y-you look just like a D-Dalmatian p-puppy." But this time he at least had the decency to turn his back so as not to spit his laughter into my face.

Finally, we both decided the job was hopeless and went to find Pa-Pa and head home. Reaching the pickup, I quickly jumped into the back with the smelly straw left by the calves we had just delivered. I felt very much at home.

Pa-Pa and my uncle both protested and told me to come ride in the cab with them since it was a long trip home. I stubbornly refused, muttering something about smelling too bad, but in reality I couldn't bear the humiliation of hearing them laugh with each retelling of the story, which I knew would reoccur every mile or so. Besides, I wanted to be alone in my resentment and anger and humiliation and plot ways to get even with them for their laughter and lack of empathy. I came up with many creative, satisfying scenarios, which, thankfully, like most of my acts of revenge over the years, never came to fruition.

With the passing of years, the story has been retold hundreds, if not thousands, of times. When two of my close friends, Tom Campbell and Tom Sublett, returned to my home on the occasion of my 15th anniversary as pastor of Walnut Hills Baptist Church in Williamsburg, Virginia, to film a humorous look at my early life, that's the first story Uncle G. A. told them. Naturally, the story came in sporadic segments, squeezed in between bursts of laughter.

Uncle G. A. and Pa-Pa are now gone to their heavenly rewards, and I alone am left to tell the story and laugh as uproariously as they did. It's a wonderful thing how the passing of time and the gaining of perspective can heal us of anger and resentment and a desire for revenge.

But, of course, as I continue my journey toward Mullinix and that fuller experience of God's grace, I've learned that we have to wait neither for the passing of time nor the gaining of perspective to be forgiving. In Ephesians we are told to "be kind and compassionate to one another, forgiving each other…just as in Christ God forgave you" (Eph 4:31–32). I'm still trying, by opening my life to God's lavish gift of grace, to "get rid of all bitterness, rage, and anger" (v. 31). An unforgiving heart so filled with resentment and bitterness has no room for anything else.

Another valuable lesson I learned that day—never squeeze a cow's tail to test its relative density.

No Crying in a Ford Pickup

I knew there was no crying in my Pa-Pa's dark green Ford pickup long before Tom Hanks dramatically informed his women's baseball team in A League of Their Own that there is "no crying in baseball." Almost as dramatically, my Pa-Pa informed me of the prohibition against crying in his pickup. And Pa-Pa knew about things that can make us cry.

Back in the mid-20s, Pa-Pa lived with his growing family in the little rural village of Midland, approximately halfway between Albemarle and Charlotte on highway 24/27 in the rolling hills of the Piedmont region of North Carolina. The family was quite comfortable there until a devastating fire completely destroyed their home and Pa-Pa's general store.

A shadow came across his face at the memory. "We lost everything," Pa-Pa said solemnly, never taking his eyes off the winding, blacktop two-lane road. "That was when I wanted to crawl into a hole and pull the hole in after me." Pa-Pa tried to chuckle because he never liked to say anything without a chuckle, but on this day the chuckle was choked down by the weight of dark memories.

Instead of digging a hole, however, Pa-Pa loaded up his young family and headed for Chip, where his parents and other relatives lived. My mother, Ina, who had just finished first grade, was deeply traumatized by that fire and carried an understandable fear of fire for the rest of her life, a fear that rises unexpectedly in my own psyche from time to time as I make a U-turn and rush home to make sure the automatic cutoff coffeepot is unplugged.

Settling in the little community of Chip, Pa-Pa and his wife, Wincie, my Ma-Ma, (with an emphasis on each syllable, just like Pa-Pa), made a new beginning, building a home across a narrow dirt road from the store Pa-Pa bought from his father, John. Great-granddaddy John had reached the time in his life where the store and post office were more than he wanted to deal with and preferred remaining as postmaster.

The Midland fire was not the last hole my Pa-Pa felt like digging. Their first son was a victim of SIDS (sudden infant death syndrome) and was found lifeless in his crib early one September morning. A second son, five-year-old Oscar, was struck down by lightning walking toward Ma-Ma as she stood on the porch next to the dirt road calling her son in for supper.

Many years later, I watched from the back seat of our family's old Dodge as my mother and her siblings exited the back door of Troy hospital at twilight, clinging to each other in deep grief. Tears sprang to my own eyes as I had assumed Ma-Ma had passed away.

I was 10 years old and had never lost anyone close to me with the exception of a black and white mixed-breed dog who was my constant companion until I found him covered with morning dew in a side ditch just to the right of our driveway on Highway 73. The school bus was just climbing the long hill to our white cinderblock house, and I was certain my grief was too great to board the bus. But that's another story.

It turned out the doctor had told them there was no hope and Ma-Ma's death from cancer was imminent. She died two days later at the young age of 56, and another hole invited Pa-Pa to climb in.

Pa-Pa was more reflective than I had ever seen him on that trip to Rockingham to deliver several crates of clucking chickens. As he shared his memories, I guess tears must have sprung to my eyes because Pa-Pa called out, "Son, you 'bout to cry? You 'bout to cry? Let me tell you about crying."

He called the name of a girl who lived on the outskirts of the Chip community whose face was severely symmetrically challenged. In his kindness, even before any of us had heard of being "politically correct," Pa-Pa refrained from calling her "ugly" as I had heard some in the community cruelly refer to her. "You know what happened to her?" And he paused dramatically until he had my full attention.

In a voice usually reserved for campfire ghost stories, Pa-Pa continued, "One real cold day—I mean real cold day—she started crying. Got real mad at her folks, the way I heard it. She cried and she cried 'til, don't you know it, her face just up and froze. Froze just like you see it today!"

Pa-Pa told the story with no malice, as if he were stating facts that could not be refuted. Even while filled with sympathy for the poor girl, I had to admit that her pinched, squinting face did look as if she were always in the middle of perpetual weeping.

So maybe the story was true.

I looked over to see if there was more to the tale, but Pa-Pa's face was red and straining with little red capillaries crisscrossing his large jowls, sure signs that he was in the middle of his signature laugh, and so I waited patiently for the explosive expiration of pent-up breath and the concluding "Ahhh, law" accompanied by a slight shaking of his head, signaling the end of his hilarity.

I guessed the story wasn't true after all.

From that time forward, however, I knew there was to be no crying in Pa-Pa's dark green Ford pickup.

After we had ridden in silence for a few more miles, Pa-Pa continued his reflections: "If I had dug that hole and pulled it in on top of me, life would have stopped, and there were too many people counting on me." After a moment's pause, Pa-Pa repeated, "There were just too many people counting on me."

During the many years since that day, a tempting array of wide, deep holes have opened before me on the way to Mullinix, all with invitations to climb in and "pull the hole in on top of me." But each time, I hear the echo of my Pa-Pa's words, which are eerily similar to Paul's words in his letters to the churches of Asia Minor: "We are troubled on every side, yet not distressed; we are perplexed, but not in despair; Persecuted, but not forsaken, cast down but not destroyed" (2 Cor 4:8–9) because "we do not grieve like the rest of those who have no hope" (1 Thess 4:13).

I would like to tell Pa-Pa that I think he was right about refusing to crawl into a hole and give up. But I would also like to tell him that I don't think he was right in not crying. Crying can be an aid in healing, rather than a sign of weakness, when our tears are filled with hope. In the words of one of my proud parishioners who broke down and wept profusely in a hospital parking lot in Richmond, Virginia, following the latest news about her husband: "Jerry, don't think I'm being weak. I cry strong!"

Along the way, we keep on, remembering there are too many people counting on us and too much life yet to be lived. We keep on, in the strength and hope rooted in the kingdom of heaven made accessible to us through Jesus Christ.

That means we can always "cry strong."

Simple Shopping

I was startled when my wife turned to me and said, "This is the best Christmas present you've ever given me." I have never been very astute at choosing the right present and usually ask my wife to select her own gifts. Handing her my Master-Card, I say, "Now get something real nice for yourself, honey."

Please understand that this isn't a dereliction of duty so much as it is the only guarantee Christmas presents will not be exchanged before a new year begins. I'm merely trying to save a step and simplify a potentially convoluted process of gift-giving.

But on this day I had not purchased anything.

We had just finished a full morning of shopping in an overcrowded outlet mall and were riding home with the back section of our Buick minivan full of skillfully selected gifts for family and friends. But what thrilled Jean the most, it seems, was that I had lasted so long.

In my marriage counseling research I had learned many years earlier that approximately 75 percent of couples choose opposites for their life partner. My wife and I are a part of that 75 percent, especially when it comes to shopping. Jean loves to shop. Wait. "Love" is not strong enough. She has a "passion" for shopping, while it takes all the intestinal fortitude I can muster to tolerate it for an hour or so.

But on this particular day I had endured longer than usual. At some point, however, Jean had noticed that my eyes had begun searching furtively for the nearest exit. My knees began to tremble slightly, and a facial tic involving my left eye and cheek suddenly appeared—a sure indication that my anxiety level was reaching a danger point. To my credit I had lasted four hours before the predict-able meltdown; surprisingly, that sacrifice was the "best gift" I had ever given her.

For a brief moment I remembered the diamond earrings and the diamond necklace and the diamond wedding ring replacement from Christmases past; each had taken me a minimum of two years to pay off. And this was the best gift? Oh, the money I could have saved by simply screwing up my courage for four hours of complaint-free shopping!

My radical aversion to shopping might have to do with a method learned at a very early age. It's a very simple, straightforward method. I simply have an item in mind, decide where I am most likely to find it, go get it, pay for it, and head back home in a maximum of 10 minutes. Shopping made simple.

No doubt my shopping method began forming around 10 years of age when I rode with my Pa-Pa in his dark green Ford pickup delivering chicken feed to the local farmers who were partnering with him in the chicken and egg business.

It didn't take long for me to discover that we were also in the clothing business. Since the chicken feed was packaged in cotton cloth with a variety of colorful patterns, these sacks were a primary source of material for the farm wives and mothers who sewed dresses and shirts for their families.

It was also one of the simplest methods of shopping ever devised. On each delivery, as we were preparing to unload the sacks of feed into the store room of the chicken house, the seamstress wife and mother would venture out and begin to look over the sacks: "Arthur, le's see if'n you got the pattern I need to finish Jessie Mae's dress."

Pa-Pa would clear his throat loudly, as he often did, either from chronic sinus drainage or allergies, and step back, giving room for the woman to amble up to the back of the canvas-covered pickup bed and look over the variety of feed sacks. After a minute or two—never more than three minutes—she would say, "There. That'un should do it. Already have two like it, and I jis' need three for this 'ticlar dress."

I would then climb into the pickup, work that sack of feed free, and step back, waiting for her to select a couple more patterns to begin her next project since this stop required three bags of feed.

Following her selection for our next delivery, she would say, "I'll need one more t'go wi' those two, Arthur. So 'member that on your nex' trip."

Satisfied with her shopping, the woman would nod her head emphatically as she stepped back from the pickup and aimed a stream of thoroughly dissolved snuff off to her right. The snuff stream landed with a decisive splat, indicating that her shopping was completed to her satisfaction.

We were on our way to the next farm in a maximum of 10 minutes.

It's a long journey from pickup-bed shopping with three or four choices on a single truck, to mall shopping with hundreds of stores containing thousands of choices.

On the way to Mullinix, the place of ultimate discipleship, we all begin the journey at different places. Some of us have much farther to travel than others, and those out ahead often find it difficult to be patient with those of us laboriously trudging behind and become critical and judgmental.

I think that's what Paul is asking us to do, however, when he wrote to the Romans, "We who are strong ought to bear with the failings of the weak" (Rom 15:1). I don't know how Paul felt about shopping, but that's a good word on the subject.

My wife has been waiting for me, in my weakness, to catch up with her strong shopping for 52 years. Neither one of us is confident I will ever make it, but a four-hour stint every two years or so is progress, I guess.

Besides, that gift of time is obviously more valuable than diamonds, and that alone makes my attempts to endure longer shopping forays a worthy undertaking.

The Right Time

As I entered the master bedroom, which doubled as a sitting room in my grandparents' home, Uncle George's sleepy eyes opened slowly, and a rare twinkle appeared in his aged eyes. The graying, unkempt head lifted almost imperceptibly from its resting place on the crooked homemade walking cane as he sought to focus on the scrawny 10-year-old pausing just inside the doorway.

A small smile appeared on the unshaven face as a still deep but no longer powerful voice uttered words I heard every time I raced through the room with my brother and cousins: "Jeremiah, Jacob, Lazarus, Paul."

We all called him "Uncle George," although he was really my great-great uncle, being the uncle of my grandfather (Pa-Pa) on my mother's side. In his younger days Uncle George was a leading citizen of the community, respectfully recognized as an educator, farmer, music teacher, justice of the peace, and information consultant long before folks started turning to Siri for answers to all their questions.

In the days before gravity became too much of a challenge, Uncle George would mount his large white horse, Bob, and ride down the winding dirt road to my grandfather's store in search of the latest newspaper or periodical. Uncle George was passionate about being well-informed on things outside the small rural community of Chip.

When my mother and her siblings had research papers due in school, the first resource they consulted was Uncle George since he was the most complete encyclopedia in their possession. Uncle George would usually go beyond their questions with challenges of his own, asking them to spell selected words and check their understanding of his answers to their inquiries.

Like many of the Haywood men on both the paternal and maternal sides of the family, Uncle George was an introvert who enjoyed his solitary existence. The peacefulness of his private life was no doubt why he was regarded as the peacemaker of the family and was uncomfortable when there was conflict.

One of Uncle George's favorite sayings as justice of the peace was, "I married many women but never had a wife." As he grew older, Uncle George probably wished he had kept one of those brides for his own.

For many years a sister cared for him, but she died several years before Uncle George, whose robust body had farmed over 300 acres twisting along Little River and was reluctant to give up.

But now Uncle George's aging body was betraying him, so he moved a mile and a half down the road to my grandparents' home. That's how it was done back then, of course. Nursing homes were neither available nor necessary since family provided the care. Being in a rural setting, someone was always around the house to care for the elderly.

In Pa-Pa and Ma-Ma's house that duty most often fell to my mother and her sisters. When Uncle George became too old to eat cornbread without choking, they took turns sitting next to him at supper, pounding on his back until the food was dislodged and everyone, including Uncle George, could breathe again. A meal of stew beef was better than a carnival game as those on the opposite side of the table dodged the missiles of meat flying toward them from the cannon of Uncle George's mouth each time it became necessary to strike his back.

I remember him mostly as a ghostly figure sitting by the little oil heater in my grandparents' front bedroom, resting his chin on the homemade walking stick, his white, drooping, untrimmed mustache encircling his work-worn bony hands.

Growing tired of hearing Uncle George complain of always being cold, Pa-Pa had driven his green Ford pickup into town, stopping at Ingram-Macauley Hardware, the only hardware store in the little village of Mt. Gilead, eight miles west of Chip. Walking into the store with purpose, Pa-Pa told Mr. Ingram, "George sits by the fireplace all day with his feet resting on the coals and still freezes. Thought I'd buy 'im a oil heater and let 'im sit astraddle of it."

Sitting beside that oil heater, rather than "astraddle" of it, was where we always found Uncle George. Most of the time, my brother and cousins ignored him as an unmoving, graying statue, part of the furniture resting just beneath the hand-carved dark walnut mantle.

I wanted desperately to ignore Uncle George like the rest of my companions since he made me uneasy with his rustic looks and brooding silence. But Uncle George would not let me ignore him.

Somehow, my name, "Jerry," triggered a fading memory of a mostly forgotten verse. Uncle George's once sharp mind had at an earlier time been filled with hundreds and probably thousands of poems and songs and sayings, which he would recite to anyone willing to listen.

My mother remembered as a small child sitting with her siblings at Uncle George's feet as he enthralled them with musical, strange words spoken in his deep, resonant voice, carrying them to strange, intriguing places unfamiliar to natives of that rural farming community.

But now there seemed to be only a faint recollection of a brief piece of verse ignited by my name. It frightened me that I had the power to awaken this shrunken giant every time I burst through the door on the way outdoors to play. How could a simple name, common at the time I was a boy, call forth that ghostly voice with the mysterious chant, "Jeremiah, Jacob, Lazarus, Paul"?

That was all. Every time, that was all. But those few words were enough to cause a satisfied nod of his large head and a throaty chuckle followed by a short cough before Uncle George's chin would drop to rest once more on his wrinkled, age-spotted hands encircling the top end of his cane.

I've searched for years to identify a song or poem or anything containing those few words with no success. I've even called in help-all in vain.

As much as that scene by the stove frightened me, I always paused until the predictable episode was completed, because we were taught to respect our elders. However, as soon as Uncle George finished his musical intonation, I smiled weakly toward him and raced out of the room with my heart beating a little faster.

Tending to bodily functions was naturally a challenge for Uncle George. Indoor plumbing was still a few years away, and for many a lot of years away, based partly on a philosophical principle.

One of the local farmers sitting around the wood stove in Pa-Pa's store spitting streams of tobacco into the sand trough surrounding the little stove was heard to remark, "Well, it's thissa here way, boys, 'bout that new-fangled indoor plumbing I hear tell 'bout." He paused then to make sure everyone was listening before he continued, "My litter of new pigs will fly away and leave their mama's teats before I take care of m' business 'n' eat under the same roof." (Of course, it would never have occurred to those earthy men of the soil to use a euphemism like "taking care of his business.") For emphasis, the speaker would then spit a larger than normal stream of tobacco toward the base of the stove, where the dark blob rested briefly before slowly seeping into the brown sand.

On the other hand, Uncle George would no doubt have welcomed indoor plumbing since his bathroom facilities were located across the dusty road running between the house and store, then up a slight hill in a field just beyond the store.

By this time, Uncle George was moving with a shuffling, side-to-side rocking motion with his almost useless feet and legs laboriously inching toward their distant destination.

One sweltering August afternoon, my great-grandfather, John, was sitting in his favorite wooden rocking chair on the long front porch attached to the west side of the house, trying to catch a rare breeze on this still day. Pulling his eyes away from the occasional passing car or mule-drawn wagon, Great-grandaddy John pushed his ever-present black derby hat a little farther up his forehead and stared at his older brother. That black derby hat was our most exciting entertainment in the days before television, as Great-granddaddy John would rapidly dance the hat up and down with his agile forehead and scalp muscles.

"George," he called out, "I had to watch for a spell to see if you was a' moving." He chuckled quietly, pulling out his large gold pocket watch with its worn gold chain to see how long it took Uncle George, after emerging from the back door of the screen porch, to move past the large chinaberry tree standing next to the oversize mailbox and reach the road.

On this particular morning, as he watched his brother's slow shuffle, Great-granddaddy John called out, "George, I just want to know one thing. It takes you 45 minutes t' reach the outhouse. How in the world d'ya know when t' start?" If he heard him at all, Uncle George didn't reply, ignoring his chuckling brother as he shuffled across the dirt road, stirring up little clouds of dust with each sliding step.

Timing. The right time. When my Uncle G. A. told me this story a couple years before his death between gasps of laughter, the way he always told a story, I could identify with Uncle George. When to start? When to stop? When to turn right or left or keep straight ahead?

I've been dramatically reminded many times that doing things at the right time is one of the keys to my successfully reaching Mullinix and experiencing the abundance of life known only to authentic citizens of God's kingdom. My journey has been slowed and even halted at crucial places along the way because of poor timing. But here's the problem according to the author of Ecclesiastes: "[God] has made everything beautiful in its time. He has also set eternity in the hearts of men, yet they cannot fathom what God has done from beginning to end" (3:11).

No wonder my timing is off! Only God knows the right time.

I don't know how successful Uncle George was in timing his jaunts to the distant outhouse correctly and how many times he may have failed. But that shuffling image always leaps into my mind whenever I hear these words: "For everything there is a season, and a time for every matter under heaven" (Eccl 3:1).

I guess that means I need to remain alert and available to God's timing at each step of my journey to Mullinix. Maybe then he can transform my untimely actions into his right time and shorten my arrival date.

A Muddy Baptism

The pastor planted his feet firmly to reestablish his precarious balance as he reached out to grasp my extended right hand. I was next in line to be baptized. But Pastor Wallace hesitated and frowned slightly as his eyes fixed on my already wet hair and dripping face. I could read his questions: "Have I already baptized this boy? Did he enjoy it so much that he sneaked back in line to have another go at it?"

The answer was much simpler and wasn't even close to my pastor's guesses.

I had been eagerly anticipating my baptism ever since I had "gone forward" at the second-week-in-August revival at Calvary Baptist Church, located out in the country near Wadeville, halfway between my hometown of Mt. Gilead and the county seat, Troy, in the Piedmont region of North Carolina.

"Going forward" or "walking the aisle" almost displaced baptism as the signature act marking the beginning of the walk with Jesus when I was a young boy. But not quite. At least not in my eyes. I had a great fear of making a display of myself by walking down the aisle—short as it was in that little rural church.

But baptism was another matter. I was eagerly anticipating my baptism. I loved rivers and creeks and branches and could hardly wait for my baptism to take place in one of those bodies where there was an abundance of water for a proper Baptist baptism. After all, John the Baptist had the whole Jordan River at his disposal.

I was deeply disappointed when the pastor and deacons decided to do something different that year. Our annual baptizing would be held in the baptistery of the First Baptist Church in Mt. Gilead, about seven miles to the west of Calvary.

I never did quite understand the reasoning behind the change. Maybe it was because we were getting ready to build a new brick church building with our own indoor baptistery and we wanted to get a feel for what it would be like. Or maybe there was a drought and the water in the river was uncommonly shallow. I was not quite 12 years old, and I had been taught to respect the decisions of my elders, whom I addressed as "sir" and "ma'am," so I did not feel it was my place to object to the chosen site for our baptism even though I was terribly disappointed. I even wondered about the validity of the whole thing, it being inside and all.

At any rate, we piled into cars and pickup trucks with our arms full of towels and dry changes of clothes. We never used robes because, according to the budget committee, they were "too expensive." I think it really had more to do with the fact that robes smacked of being too high church for us simple folk. According to one respected Calvary theologian, "What good would it do for us to be baptized in humility on one hand and on the other hand be so uppity as to wear robes and refill our just emptied hearts with false pride?" Well, anyone could see it wouldn't work.

But off we went to the First Baptist Church of Mt. Gilead for our baptizing in a highfalutin' indoor baptistery.

My brother, Kent, and several of my cousins had "come forward" on the same night I had, so we were all going to be baptized together. The Holy Spirit often has a way of invading an entire family at the same time.

I should have said something about wanting a river baptism even if I was only 12, because when we reached the church and walked through the unlocked door—this was back before the sad day when we felt it necessary to begin locking our church doors—we knew immediately that something was wrong. There was no smell of water. Folks who grew up next to rivers and branches knew what water smelled like. This was not it.

One of the older boys who had been baptized a couple years earlier and was therefore an expert on the whole matter came running down the green-carpeted center aisle from the front of the church, calling out, "They ain't no water!"

"Whatta ya mean?" asked the startled pastor. Squaring his shoulders, the previously baptized teenager said importantly, "They ain't a dang drop of water in that air baptizin' tub. Not nary a drop."

We started looking at each other wondering what was going to happen next as the pastor gathered a tight circle of deacons around him. Things felt a little uneasy, but I was confident that a pastor standing in the center of a circle of lifetime deacons could solve anything.

I crept just close enough to overhear one of the deacons say, "I knowed it warn't gonna work. Jesus were baptized in a river, and I never saw no need t'change the way the good Lord hisself done it."

With that he plopped his brown Sunday hat on his shiny bald head, lifted his chin, and walked through the front door letting it slam behind him.

I was glad that wasn't the last word, although this particular man always thought there was nothing else to be said after he had spoken, placed his hat on his head, and slammed the door behind him. I had watched that scene play out before our good folks for years. At our home church, however, this particular man would place his hat on the piano so everyone could see him clearly when he made public what the Lord had told him privately "in his heart."

As soon as this deacon would finish proclaiming his "word from the Lord," which he always assumed no one would accept, he quickly stood, strode to the piano, plopped his brown dress hat on his hairless head, and marched by the large potbelly toward the front door, which, as I said, he always slammed on the way out.

Here at First Baptist, he had placed his hat on the back pew since there was no piano available when he entered; thus, the entire scene lost some of its usual impact. That was my first lesson in conflict resolution within the church. Since then, I have both studied and taught classes in healthy conflict resolution, so I'm a little disappointed when the "hat on the piano" technique remains so popular.

Several bodies of water were mentioned as potential locations for our baptism since none of us wanted to call it off, what with our arms already full of towels and dry clothes. Finally, someone came up with the name of a Mr. Thompson who had a large fish pond on the winding blacktop road about halfway between Mt. Gilead and my Pa-Pa's home in Chip.

So that's how we ended up on the banks of a muddy fish pond. All of us baptismal "candidates" gathered about halfway down on the left side of the fish pond while the choir members took their places near the north end next to the road.

I was feeling better all the time. I especially loved fish ponds and felt at home. Everything had turned out great, and I was excited for what was to come—until the pastor and a couple deacons waded out cautiously to find a place with the proper depth for the baptizing.

That was when I saw swirls of blackish, brackish water rising to the surface with each tentative step. When the pastor slipped and grabbed a deacon's arm to remain upright, I knew we were in trouble. My brother and I took a couple short steps into the edge of the water and sank at least three inches in slimy mud. That was just at the edge of the pond. What awaited us in the deeper water?

Finally, we noticed that the pastor and deacons had stopped, supposedly satisfied that this was the best place. I was third in line as we slowly walked toward the pastor, his exuberant smile replaced with a worried, forced little grin. It was obvious that he was mighty anxious about baptizing this group of rowdy boys standing in slippery mud, but it was too late to back out now.

As he reached for one of my first cousins, I heard the choir slide into our traditional hymn of baptism, "Shall We Gather at the River?" Hunter Sedberry, about the only one of our group who wasn't a cousin—and maybe he was if we had looked hard enough, which none of us wanted to do—whispered to me, "This here ain't no river. It's a dang muddy fish pond."

Turning slightly, I told him to hush. This was a sacred baptism, and my mother wouldn't even let us say "gosh," so to hear him say "dang" at such a holy moment filled me with a little shiver of fear that he might negate the whole process.

But our choir was not about to change the words to allow for a muddy fish pond: "Shall we gather at the river, where bright angel feet have trod, with its crystal tide forever, flowing by the throne of God?"

The thought struck me that I would hate to see this muddy water flowing by the throne of Almighty God, but I was now second in line and had to put such thoughts out of my head.

"Soon we'll reach the shining river; soon our pilgrimage will cease." I could see that my pilgrimage toward baptism was quickly ceasing as the pastor was extending his hand as I stood dripping before him.

I prayed the pastor's baptism wouldn't be anticlimactic since I had already been dunked twice before reaching him. However, since the cousin who had pulled me out of the water when my feet slipped from under me was not ordained, I was pretty sure it didn't count in the eyes of the Lord.

Just as the pastor grabbed my hand, however, I felt him hesitate and turn toward the north end of the pond where the choir was standing. I followed his gaze and noticed the choir's harmony had been disturbed by a restless shuffling and the sudden silence of some choir members.

Only one clear voice was still discernible. A familiar deep bass voice was confidently belting out the names of the shape notes: "Fa, sol, me, sol, la, ti, do, do, do, do."

Our lead bass singer, who sometimes had trouble reading the words and notes all at the same time, would often concentrate on the names of the notes learned at one of our annual church music schools. But he, too, seemed unusually distracted. I was startled to learn why. While holding his Stamps-Baxter song book in his right hand, his left hand was desperately clinging to the dress tail of an alto in front of him.

That was mighty mysterious to me since I had never noticed any fooling around in our choir. So I was relieved to see that the plump alto was standing precariously on the edge of the slick muddy bank, in danger of slipping into the water at any moment.

But our reliable bass's grip was firm, and I knew the dress would hold because it was made out of one of the cotton print chicken feed sacks my Pa-Pa and I delivered to the various farms around Chip. It was virtually impossible to tear one of those sacks, so I figured the alto would stay dry if the gallant bass's grip remained firm. Unfortunately, some of the sopranos up front were already up to their ankles in the soft mud.

Later, I discovered that a water moccasin, unaccustomed to sacred services in his home pond, had slithered across the bank a few feet from the choir, initiating the present chaos. At our next Wednesday night prayer meeting, one biblical scholar suggested that the snake was merely carrying on the family business of wreaking havoc in the lives of good folk, a business first established in the garden of Eden.

I reluctantly pulled my eyes away from the shuffling choir, worried that Satan was working mighty hard to invalidate my baptism. Such thoughts disappeared, however, when pastor Wallace lifted his right hand toward heaven, tightly clutching the wet handkerchief he would momentarily slap over my face, and intoned solemnly, "Brother Haywood, in obedience to the command of our Lord and Savior, Jesus Christ, and upon your profession of faith in him, I baptize you in the name of the Father and of the Son and of the Holy Ghost."

The last sound I heard before slipping beneath the muddy water and the roar of water in my ears drowning all other noises was that rich bass voice belting out the shape notes made popular for the modern world by Julie Andrews in The Sound of Music.

I was disappointed that only the notes and not the words of that traditional hymn were sung at my baptism. I wanted everything to be perfect, and the whole thing was permeated with imperfection.

My sense of discouragement was quickly dispelled, however, when the pastor lifted me out of the water and I blinked away the remnants of the muddy water. Looking up as the last drops of filthy water drained from my eyes, I was surprised to gaze into the clearest, bluest sky I can ever remember seeing.

As the pastor handed me off to the deacon assigned to help us back to shore, I was lost in the wonder of how it was possible to emerge from muddy, dirty water into one of the cleanest scenes in my bank of memories.

But I guess that's what faith is really all about: "You were taught, with regard to your former way of life, to put off your old self, which is being corrupted by its deceitful desires; to be made new in the attitude of your mind; and to put on the new self, created to be like God in true righteousness and holiness" (Eph 4:22–24).

I think of my baptism often on the way to Mullinix, that symbolic place of perfect discipleship, and it helps me through the places of dirty waters and deep, slippery mud, threatening to suck me under.

The sun will break through eventually, and the old will be in the past, and the new will be waiting up ahead.

In the Heart of a Child

"**S**on, you look hot. Get you a drink from the drink box."

My Pa-Pa's words were like an invitation to walk through the pearly gates for a 10-year-old boy whose shirtless torso was dripping large beads of sweat, turning his thin, dust-covered body into a walking mud puddle.

I had just raced up the narrow, dusty dirt road between Pa-Pa's house and his country store, "Haywood's Grocery," according to the large sign over the white double front doors. So reaching into the drink box for a Nehi grape drink, resting up to its neck in slowly circulating ice cold water, I was transported onto an oasis in the desert of a hot North Carolina August day.

The large sign over the front doors was really unnecessary since the store was the commercial and social center of the little community of Chip and was well-known by everyone. In fact, the store was Chip, having required a name back when it also served as the local post office.

The store was built somewhere around 1910–1912 by Pa-Pa's father, John Haywood, who also served as the postmaster. Finding it difficult to operate both the post office and the general store, my great-granddaddy sold the store to his son, George Arthur Haywood Sr., my Pa-Pa, somewhere in the mid-1920s.

Sadly, the post office part of the store closed in the late 1930s when the federal post office folks decided to begin rural free delivery and Route 3 was born. The little community Chip post office became a relic, used by Pa-Pa as his office with its large roll-top desk enclosed within a two-foot tall wooden picket fence.

My favorite place in the store was the feed room attached to the right side of the store as you faced it. Filled to capacity with feed for animals of all kinds, especially chickens, it was a buffet of pungent aromas, which I found homey and comforting.

The chicken feed in particular smelled good enough to eat, but like my experience with Red Man chewing tobacco, I only tried it once. On that momentous tasting day I learned the valuable lesson that what is pleasant to your nose does not necessarily belong in your mouth. That lesson has served me well through the years as I have gloried in the pleasurable smell of vanilla flavoring, honeysuckle vines, and cherry smoking tobacco, all of which seriously fail the taste test.

My next favorite place in that little country store was sitting by the little wood stove surrounded by a rectangle box full of brown sand into which the farmers spit their chewing tobacco juice during their rare offseason idle hours. The stove sat near the rear of the store next to the white fence enclosing the former post office.

From a very young age I preferred listening to the stories of grownups rather than playing with children my own age. However, sitting with folks 40 years my senior also made me the target of much kidding. Most of it was good-natured, and I laughed along with them so long as their miscalculation of my intelligence did not seriously compromise my self-respect.

One day, however, I made the mistake of casually remarking that their spitting seemed "mighty accurate," hitting the sandbox every time instead of splattering on the wooden floor. That was a very good thing since my Pa-Pa was fastidious when it came to cleanliness.

Pa-Pa always wore a clean, carefully ironed medium-brown uniform, which today would be called "khaki" but I knew as "brown" in rural North Carolina. The shirt pocket had a plastic pocket guard emblazoned with the logo of a variety of animal feed companies, which Pa-Pa rotated when one became smudged with ink or stained with tobacco from his ever-present pack of Lucky Strikes.

What a hailstorm a careless, throwaway comment can sometimes provoke! Little did I know that mentioning their accuracy would give birth to one of the longest-running "jokes" in Chip folklore.

"Ya think tha's accurate?" one of the overalls-wearing tobacco chewers asked with wide, excited eyes. Rising so quickly that his wooden cane-bottomed chair almost fell backward, he took two long strides until he hovered over me. "Boy, I c'n spit all the way 'crost this here store through that 'air keyhole on th' front door and git nary a splatter on th' white paint." The roar of laughter convinced the speaker that he had suddenly become one of the cleverest men in the county. From that day forward, he could not let it go.

Invoking laughter can become a serious addiction as I later learned while watching a number of my sermons deteriorate into an attempt to elicit laughter from folks thirsty for a word from the Lord. Laughter and a word from the Lord are not antithetical, of course. Far from it. The Bible is full of humor, and laughter can lead many reluctant souls into an experience of grace. But addictions of all kinds can quickly cause a person to lose perspective, as it did that farmer many years ago.

Thoroughly enjoying being the center of attention, the middle-aged farmer with a scruffy, two-day-old gray-flecked black beard stained at the corners of his mouth with tobacco juice would not drop his attempt to entertain his audience by testing the credibility of a shy, 10-year-old country boy with a cold Nehi grape drink held tightly between his legs, resting on the cane-bottomed chair.

Standing with his thumbs hooked carelessly in the bib of his Lee overalls, the farmer persisted in a voice rising with excitement, "Whatta ya say, boy? Think I c'n do it?"

When I responded with a weak smile, he turned toward the door and pretended to ready his tobacco juice for a mighty hurl. I remained silent. Pausing just before actually spitting, he sat back down, laughing raucously as if that was the funniest thing he had ever done. It probably was.

Thus began a two-year weekly rerun of that scene: same words, same actions, and same response from his audience. Maybe that was the beginning of my strong distaste for repetition. In my early years as a pastor, I would occasionally hear people say, "You better listen carefully because Jerry won't repeat himself."

When I later learned how many times an individual needs to hear something before it penetrates their overload of information, I guess I should have paid more attention to the value of repetition. I learned early, however, how downright boring and annoying repetition can be.

I didn't mind being the butt of their jokes nearly as much as I was offended by their assumption that I was oblivious to what was really happening. If only they knew how many secrets they revealed through their body language, the tone of their voice, the expressions on their face, a careless word, all easy to read through my silent observations. If they had had a clue of how much I knew about their personal lives, they would either shoot me or never allow me to sit around the tobacco juice-splattered sandbox again.

I've noticed most folks greatly underestimate the intelligence and perception of children, sometimes ignoring them as if they were not in the room or regarding them as pieces of furniture or as nuisances to be chased away.

Seems even the disciples thought part of their job description was to protect Jesus from the bothersome presence of children, driving away those parents who wanted their children to sit in Jesus' presence.

But Jesus said, "Let the little children come to me, and do not hinder them, for the kingdom of heaven belongs to such as these" (Matt 19:14).

I wish I could have seen the disciples' faces when they asked Jesus about who was going to be greatest in the kingdom of heaven. It would have been a hoot to watch them bow their red faces and shift from foot to foot when Jesus invited a little child to step into their exclusive adult circle and said, "I tell you the truth: unless you change and become like little children, you will never enter the kingdom of heaven" (Matt 18:3).

I remember my own startled reaction when, many years later, I spoke to an eight-year-old boy at the request of his parents. The little fellow had developed the dangerous habit of racing across a busy highway to retrieve his soccer ball. Warning him as gently as I could about the consequences of being hit by a car, my heart constricted and a shiver ran up my spine when he answered, "That's okay. Sometimes I think I'd like to go back to heaven. It's been a while since I saw God." Then his eyes suddenly widened in alarm as he looked at me and said, "Don't tell Mama and Daddy."

I never did because it was obvious the little fellow did not have a death wish. The words were spoken innocently and naturally as only one can who has an intimate knowledge and personal experience of God's nearness.

Heaven was as close and comforting to this little boy as his daily experience of God's presence in his life. In his trusting heart, this world and the next were separated only by a transparent curtain through which he could walk with one small child's step. So I kept his secret, wishing we were all more like him.

Many debates have been waged over the particular quality of a child Jesus had in mind when he said we must change and become like little children. Was he referring to a child's trust, humility, dependence? The list of attributes goes on and on, most of which are foreign to the children I know.

I've often wondered if maybe Jesus was talking about a child's innate ability to notice and intuitively understand God and the world around him or her far greater than adults, who are hardened by time and experience and skepticism. Perhaps the child's ability to be aware and open to God's presence is the true key to the kingdom of heaven.

Looking back, why should I have expected those farmers to understand my abilities of discernment when even Jesus' disciples had no clue and were looking everywhere for the kingdom except in the heart of a child? Maybe while "going to Mullinix," that place of the fullest experience of the kingdom come to earth, I need to notice when a child suddenly appears and follow.

The Last Corn-shucking

I was not old enough to enter first grade at the elementary school in my hometown of Mt. Gilead, North Carolina, when Pa-Pa held the last of his annual corn-shuckings.

Today I would be called a preschooler, but back then I was just one more young'un too small to be of any 'count at real labor like shucking corn. So I just wandered around, awed by all the frenetic activity coming from the base of the mountain of unshucked corn snaking around the corn crib that rested maybe 100 feet down a gentle slope from the open front door of my Pa-Pa's large barn.

Oh, it was better than a circus when the shucked corn started flying over the semicircle of unshucked corn, little yellow rockets streaking through the growing twilight. The launching sites were the skillful, work-toughened hands of the farmers and neighbors who sat on cinderblock-supported thick oak boards wide enough to comfortably accommodate the broad bottoms of the shuckers.

As darkness closed in, the hill of shucked corn grew steadily higher until it was peeking over the top of the unshucked corn piled nearer the shuckers. The enveloping darkness also increased the volume of the muted conversations and the warmth of that intimate, special laughter known only among longtime friends who have fought together to eke a living out of the soil against the common enemies of changing weather, the invasion of insects, and other threats to their crops.

In my meanderings behind the low board benches, I heard some of the grownups telling how some corn-shucking hosts would stick a bottle of whiskey in the pile of corn to encourage haste and perseverance as eager hands sought the prize. Still others, they said, would throw in a few red ears here and there. The man lucky enough to find a red ear could kiss the woman of his choice.

My grandfather never resorted to such motivational tactics. Pa-Pa was a teetotaler, and he "reckoned there was already too much fooling around" in the rural farming community surrounding Chip.

But the truth is that there was no need for such tricks to make the people show up and work hard. My grandmother's chicken and dumplings took care of that.

Folks would go in shifts of a dozen or so at a time to lift their stiffening bodies from the benches and put their feet under Ma-Ma's table, eating their fill before heading back to reclaim their places before the dwindling hill of unshucked corn.

Ma-Ma had only one requirement. You had better come to her table with clean hands, carefully scrubbed in the pan of well water, frequently changed, on the back porch shelf. A large bar of homemade lye soap rested beside the pan. Everyone felt that was a small price to pay for Ma-Ma's chicken and dumplings—except Buford Johnson.

Buford was his generation's version of a homeless person. In reality Buford had several homes scattered around the countryside, sleeping from barn to barn wherever there was handyman work to be done. The work, no matter how small, lasted a long time because Buford was slow walking and slow talking and slow working.

Pa-Pa figured Buford only shucked about a dozen ears of corn a night, but Ma-Ma was generous and kindhearted and would turn no one away from her table. That is, if they carefully scrubbed their hands.

My mother, next to the oldest of the six surviving children, carried on the twin traditions of inviting everyone to her table and of having a passion for cleanliness. One day I noticed her rinsing (we called it "wrenching") paper plates, which she was preparing to throw in the trash. "Why in the world are you doing that, Mother?" I asked. "Well," she replied while continuing her rinsing, "I don't like the garbage to get too messy."

Ma-Ma was a small, quiet woman whose deeply lined face revealed the lingering pain of losing two sons, one through sudden infant death syndrome and the other struck by lightning. That last trauma sent Ma-Ma to bed, where she remained for a long time, unable even to attend five-year-old Oscar's funeral.

As nonconfrontational as she was, Ma-Ma would always stand up to Buford when it came to hand washing. Oh, it was quite a show, that annual struggle between Ma-Ma and Buford, and I always followed him into the house so I wouldn't miss it. Buford would try to sneak up to the table while Ma-Ma's back was turned as she stirred the chicken and dumplings on the wood-burning cook stove. But she always recognized Buford's slow shuffle as he crept up to ease his chair back from the table.

"Buford," Ma-Ma would say quietly without turning around, "the wash pan's on the porch."

"Welllll, Mizzz Winncieee," Buford would drawl, "don' b'lieve m' hans is dirrr-rty." He would wipe them slowly up and down the front of his soiled bib overalls.

"Buford, you may think that, but ever'body washes before they eat my chicken and dumplings." Turning from the stove, she would continue, "And while you at it, wash your face a little."

Buford's face was perpetually covered with scruffy white whiskers with just a smattering of black hairs desperately clinging to the remnants of his last meal, usually smears of Peter Pan peanut butter purchased from Pa-Pa's store just across the narrow dirt road. Thin slices of cheese from the hoop sitting at the end of the counter on the left as you walked into the fragrant country store and peanut butter were Buford's main diet. Occasionally, someone would give him a plug of Red Man chewing tobacco, which left dark stains at the corners of Buford's mouth, leaking down in parallel thin lines to the bottom of his chin. Completing his distinctive look, Buford placed a fraying railroad cap on top of his graying blond hair, which rivaled his beard for scruffiness.

This annual exchange between Ma-Ma and Buford would go on for several minutes before Buford's hunger would overcome his aversion to cleanliness and he would shuffle out to the porch, splashing the clean basin water around noisily in a great show of washing. As he reentered the kitchen, Ma-Ma was standing in the doorway to examine the hands Buford reluctantly held out with palms down. "Turn 'em over so I can see the other side, Buford," Ma-Ma would say.

Sometimes she would send him back to try again with Buford grumbling all the way. Other times she would realize that Buford had done the best he could and let him pass with final instruction: "Now don' forget to take your cap off at the table."

It was quite a show, this tug of war between Buford and Ma-Ma, my favorite part of the whole corn-shucking circus. But I think that tussle, carved indelibly into my block of childhood memories, is the primary cause of my present squeamishness every time I come face to face with a pot of chicken and dumplings. As good as they smell and taste, I can't get the image of those little white bits of dumplings clinging to the corners of Buford's mouth, held into place for days to come by his gray chin whiskers.

Some memories can damage a person for life.

In spite of his shortcomings, Buford did have at least one thing in common with Jesus. Of course, he may have had many more Christ-like traits unrecognized by my casual observations. During my many years as a pastor to all kinds of people, I've noticed failure to find Jesus in unlikely individuals often happens, and that's why I try to leave all judgments to God.

I do know for a fact, however, that Jesus refused to wash his hands on occasion. As far as I know, he didn't show up at any corn-shuckings; at least, I didn't see Jesus at my Pa-Pa's last corn-shucking. But again, I've missed noticing him on many other occasions and can't speak authoritatively on the subject of Jesus sightings.

Maybe he didn't make it to any corn-shuckings, but Jesus did seem to eat out a lot. One day he was invited to eat at the house of a Pharisee. Jesus accepted the invitation but then reclined at the table without washing his hands.

The Pharisees were as unhappy as my grandmother would have been, even if it was Jesus. Not only did the Pharisees think a person ought to wash his hands in a carefully prescribed manner before eating, but hands were expected to be washed between each course. That was even more washing than my grandmother required. Ma-Ma never sent Buford out to wash between the chicken and dumplings and her signature banana pudding. Thank goodness I still love creamy banana pudding in spite of Buford's facial leftovers.

Jesus' reasons for not washing, however, were far different from Buford's aversion to cleanliness. Jesus did not dislike cleanliness, only the false appearance of cleanliness. He could not abide hypocrisy and what the Pharisees thought made you clean. They believed if you washed the outside, you were entirely clean and a good person, meeting all the necessary requirements for pleasing God.

They were eternally wrong: "Now you Pharisees cleanse the outside of the cup and dish, but inside you are full of extortion and wickedness. You fools! Did not he who made the outside make the inside also?" (Luke 11:39–41).

Self-deception and self-righteousness are major stumbling blocks on the way to Mullinix—huge, looming threats to growth in kingdom living. Every time I begin to feel comfortable about my small attempts at goodness, I remember Buford and his futile splashing of a half-full basin of well water over stubborn, ground-in dirt that never quite surrendered to his halfhearted efforts.

That's when I am brought face to face with the hard realization that even an overflowing basin of right living will not be nearly enough to cleanse my soiled insides. If I'm going to make it to Mullinix, I must stand empty-handed with palms up under a lavish, rushing waterfall of God's grace.

Part Two

Intriguing Characters

Grand Canyon Cowboy

When we arrived in the parking lot of El Tovar, the historic hotel located just a few feet from the South Rim of the Grand Canyon, my wife, Jean, immediately began unloading our luggage. But I couldn't wait for my first look at that wonder of creation and walked toward the stone wall.

However, I hadn't expected my first look to be this.

First, before you think too unkindly of me for heading off while my wife was doing all the heavy lifting, let me explain. Jean grew up in Washington, DC, and she moves at a much faster pace than I, having grown up in the Piedmont region of North Carolina. For instance, when a thought enters her mind, Jean acts on it immediately. In rural North Carolina I learned to let a thought sit on my mind for two or three days before being moved to action.

Jean is, therefore, much more productive than I am, but sometimes, moving at a slower pace, I have a better chance of seeing what's going on around me. At least that's what I tell myself to assuage the occasional bouts of guilt over moving at train speed while Jean is in plane mode.

So while Jean was unloading the luggage, my eye caught sight of a disheveled man in his early middle years dangling his feet over the stone wall of that section of the canyon with nothing beneath but the seemingly infinite depths of that great canyon.

Rushing over to him, I called out, "Isn't that a little dangerous?" He turned to me slowly and grinned even more slowly. I immediately felt a kinship with him as one who could also let a thought sit on his mind for two or three days before acting on it.

"Naw," he replied in a soft southern drawl. "I'm from Tennessee." He stared at me silently as if that was the only explanation I needed.

His deeply lined face, which probably was quite handsome in an earlier period of his life, was now covered with several days' growth of a slightly graying beard, succeeding in hiding only a few of those lines. A cigarette dangled from the right corner of his mouth and a half-empty bottle of Jack Daniels rested carelessly between his long, faded jeans-covered legs. The old jeans perfectly matched his well-worn denim shirt.

Continuing to stare at me through bleary eyes beneath a white Stetson hat turned a mottled gray from long use and little cleaning, he spoke slowly, causing the cigarette to bounce gently between his lips.

"I'm from Tennessee" he repeated. "Mountains of Tennessee." His head turned toward the canyon. "But I ain't never seen nothin' like this."

For the first time my attention was drawn to that remarkable phenomenon, one of the real wonders in a wondrous world. "Unbelievable," I gasped as I stared into the canyon, feeling drawn to this stranger in that sudden kinship created by shared awe. My spine tingled, and I was momentarily rendered speechless.

Finally, he muttered softly as one afraid of speaking too loudly in church, "God shore done a good job wi' that, din' he?"

"He shore did," I replied, falling easily into my native North Carolina vernacular.

"I'm from the mountains of Tennessee," he said for the third time. "Big mountains. But I ain't never seen nothin' like this." Another pause. "Called m' mama, tried to tell 'er 'bout it. Sister too. Couldn' find the words. They jus' din' unnerstand."

I understood that. An experience of extreme awe often carries us beyond our previous experience of the world and reveals something so new and marvelous that we are rendered speechless—or at the very least unable to find the right words.

My new friend reached into the pocket of his denim shirt and slowly pulled out a pack of Marlboros, causing me to wonder briefly if I was standing in the presence of the original cowboy in those "Marlboro Man" commercials so popular some years back. Suddenly, he remembered the cigarette he had stuck behind his left ear and slipped it out to place between his chapped lips. Almost in the same motion, he brushed the butt he had crushed a moment earlier on the rock wall into his palm and carefully transferred the cooling bits of scorched tobacco and gray ashes into his jeans pocket.

"Some things you have to see for yourself," I said. "Some things you can't even imagine."

We were silent for another few minutes. Finally, he muttered out of the side of his mouth so quietly that this time the cigarette did not even move, "It's a wondrous thang."

About that time, another wonder began to creep into my mind. I'm not sure what I expected. Maybe that my first glimpse of this unimaginable wonder of nature would be accompanied by King David appearing behind me to recite one of his psalms of creation: "The heavens declare the glory of God; the skies proclaim the work of his hands" (Ps 19:1).

Or perhaps I wanted the Mormon Tabernacle Choir to burst from behind the stone wall with a rousing rendition of Handel's "Hallelujah Chorus."

I don't know what I expected. But it certainly wasn't having a slightly intoxicated mountain man from Tennessee usher me into a worship experience exceeding most I had previously experienced. I have always felt that awe is the deepest form of worship. Awe transports us into the presence of one much larger than ourselves. True awe possesses the power to draw us out of the little "me" into the infinite "we."

I'm not sure what I expected. But I was deeply grateful for the unexpected experience of shared awe with a fellow pilgrim.

It was also a good reminder that not all signs pointing to Mullinix are clearly marked. Some of them are just as faded and uncertain as that first sign my Pa-Pa came across long years before. God's signs of his presence often occur in surprising places in surprising, unlikely people.

Paul told us a long time ago that "we have this treasure in jars of clay to show that the all-surpassing power is from God and not from us" (2 Cor 4:7).

I made a mental note to remember that on my journey to Mullinix—that place where I am more clearly marked with the stripes of Christ—the route is often indicated through faces that outwardly don't resemble him a great deal but still reflect an inner light if the eyes of my heart are alert to see.

Turning back toward El Tovar, I noticed that my wife had stacked all our luggage before the front door, impatiently waiting for me to come sign in. So I reluctantly told my new brother goodbye and turned to resume our journey through the magnificent sights of the West.

As I did so, I was keenly aware that my personal journey toward becoming Christ to the world had also just passed another milepost.

POSTSCRIPT: The next Sunday morning in church, I described this Grand Canyon cowboy while relating our experiences through the West, a trip the church had generously provided for us on the occasion of our 30th anniversary serving Walnut Hills. A young woman in her late 20s rushed up at the conclusion of our worship with wide eyes and flushed face, exclaiming, "Pastor! I think you found my daddy!" As our laughter subsided, I said, "Maybe I did. I just may have. The world is full of mysteries we cannot even imagine."

Redneck Angel on Interstate 95

The hurricane-like wind, driving the rain sideways, was rapidly loosening my inexperienced knots and stripping away the blue tarp covering the furniture and assorted household goods on the back of our borrowed pickup.

Frantically, I leaped from the warm cab and began a desperate attempt to retie the ropes I had threaded through the corner and side holes of the waterproof tarp. Completely focused on the hopeless task, I was startled to feel a hand on my left shoulder, gently but firmly pushing me aside.

My wife and I were returning to our home in Williamsburg, Virginia, from Fredericksburg, Virginia, where friends had relocated and had some extra stuff they thought would help us furnish our newly constructed home.

Realizing that if the tarp were to blow off completely, all our stuff would be ruined, I eased off Interstate 95 onto a wide shoulder and began a futile attempt to secure the knots. My heart sank as I saw that the rear left corner of the tarp had come completely loose and in its unrestrained flapping was in the process of ripping the right corner loose.

"Why hadn't I stayed with the Boy Scouts more than one meeting?" I muttered to myself. "At least until we had the class on knot-tying."

In my defense, at that initial meeting the Scoutmaster never showed up, and the whole affair quickly degenerated into a rowdy, unsupervised wrestling match. I could get that every day during recess at Mt. Gilead Elementary School, where this meeting was also being held.

Now, someone who had evidently stayed with the Scouts or served a stint in the Navy or hauled freight cross country in a 10-wheeler rig was firmly pushing me aside and with skilled fingers began retying the knots, which even to my untrained eyes promised to hold fast against the unforgiving elements.

Peeping beneath the hood of my light jacket, I made out a shadowy figure through the almost zero visibility of the sideways-driven rain. The man's features were mostly obscured by a ragged John Deere cap pulled so low it touched the upturned collar of his light jacket, even more ineffective than mine against the raging storm.

As I moved closer to my rescuer, he turned slightly while still skillfully tying the knots and began shouting in my ear. I strained to hear, realizing he was telling his story.

"Used to be an alcoholic," he cried breathlessly, straining on the knots. Speaking in short phrases, he continued relating a story I had heard many times as a pastor. But even though the situations were often the same, the conclusion and the response in each story were as unique as the individual.

"Los' ever'thin'. M' wife. M' house. M' friends." The man paused briefly as he moved over to fasten the right corner. "Stopped by one o' them downtown missions in Balt'more. Good preacher that night." He was breathing harder as he struggled to pull the ropes tighter over the top of the wildly wriggling tarp.

"Give m' life t' Jesus," he said with a short grunt of exertion. "Give 'im ever'thin' I had, which shore won't much," he added with a slight chuckle. "But I guess it were enough fer 'im to do summat with."

With one last tug to make sure the knot was secure, he concluded his story: "Now I jus' drive up and down this here road t' look fer somebody to he'p."

"You sure saved my bacon!" I hollered into his ear while holding out a 10-dollar bill. He pushed it away quickly with a frown as if I had insulted him.

"No, no," he said. "'Preciate it, but taking that money'd squeeze all the joy outn'it."

Holding out his hand, which I shook enthusiastically, he shouted over his shoulder as he turned back to his own beat-up pickup. "Preacher told me things like this'll stretch m' soul." Again, he chuckled, "Shore done a good job a-shrinkin' it most o' m' life."

Pausing briefly to watch him walk away, even though the rain was still hammering down on me, I wondered if there were a class of interstate redneck angels who wore beat-up John Deere caps and ragged olive green windbreakers instead of halos.

"Did you pay him?" my wife asked as I climbed back into the cab. "Said he didn't want it. God always gave him all he needed."

As I pulled back into the storm-slowed interstate traffic, I reflected on another passing encounter that took place beside a well where a thirsty woman had come to draw water and unexpectedly met a man who offered her a deep drink of grace. John set the stage for this encounter: "Now he had to go through Samaria" (John 4:4).

Geographically speaking, Jesus did not have to go through Samaria. Even though it was the most direct route, Jewish travelers usually tried to avoid the land of the hated Samaritans, so when John says Jesus "had to go through Samaria," he must have been talking about a spiritual compulsion to travel that way—like when Jesus stopped to heal the blind man or when he paused in the middle of a shoving crowd to ask, "Who touched me?" Or the day he restored a dead son to his mother. Over and over again, it seems Jesus "had" to show up where he was needed most.

The only satisfactory answer to these compulsions is that Jesus was always willing to obey his Father's voice. So maybe I wasn't far from the truth when I wondered if a redneck angel had visited us along Interstate 95 on that stormy day—or, if not an angel, at least a disciple who bore the distinctive marks of a kingdom citizen making his arduous way through an alien world.

Back in 1969 folks kept telling our small community of believers meeting in an elementary school cafeteria that we would never erect a place of worship on the ravine-scarred piece of land lying beside Jamestown Road. But we had to build. A compulsion, which we firmly believed originated with God, drove us to show up and meet a need.

Perhaps I'm drawing nearer Mullinix, that higher plane of kingdom citizenship, when I readily respond to those compulsions to show up when I sense a voice calling to me.

Smelling Like Easter

"Jerry!" the voice on the other end of the phone cried. She sounded panicky. "I need your help. I am literally freaked out!"

From time to time I receive calls from parishioners who have moved away, often to another state. I received one of those calls on Easter Sunday evening some years ago from a young woman who was not only a former member of our church but had also been a neighbor.

She would wander over from time to time when she would see me working in the yard. In her mind it was a particularly good time to engage me in deep theological discussions on thorny issues when I was blowing leaves.

On this particular Easter Sunday evening when my former neighbor called from several states south of Virginia, it was obvious she was frightened. "I just had the most unusual experience, and it's left me shaken." Her voice trembled as she continued, "A young boy, 13, walked up to me in church today and said that I smelled like Easter."

"Well," I said jovially in a somewhat insensitive attempt to calm her anxiety, "after all, it is Easter. If you're going to smell like Easter, this is the day to do it."

"Jerry, I'm serious," she replied quickly, annoyed at my misguided attempt to make light of the situation. "This has freaked me out! What did he mean?"

"I don't know," I replied, trying hard to match the gravity of her tone. "What kind of perfume did you wear?"

"Why are you asking about my perfume?" She was really growing irritated with me now, but the numerous services of Holy Week had taken a lot out of me, and I wasn't sure I was up to this.

"Well," I continued, "maybe your perfume reminded him of Easter lilies. Or maybe it smelled sweet like those candy Easter eggs with a hard shell and marshmallow on the inside." Pausing for a brief moment, I hurried on, "Or, heaven forbid, he did not like your perfume, and it reminded him of dyed Easter eggs kept so long they start to smell or…"

"Jerry, I'm serious!" she yelled into the phone, causing my wife, sitting across the room, to look up and frown. "This has really scared me!"

"Smelling like Easter has frightened you?" I replied, employing a favorite counseling technique that gives me time to think of what to say next. I told you I was tired.

"He's a strange kid," she hurried on. "Every time he says something unusual, something weird happens to me."

"And now you're afraid Easter might happen to you?"

It was obvious she wasn't listening, which made me wonder briefly if I might as well have left the leaf blower running during all our previous conversations.

Finally, she came to the thing that was really bothering her. "Do you think he smelled death on me?"

"Wait a minute! Wait just a minute!" Now I was yelling into the phone. My wife's puzzled frown was growing deeper. "Easter is about life. Didn't you listen to the sermon today? Or did you just show up out of obligation?" We had always been able to talk straight with each other, and this was not the first time I had questioned her motivations for attending church.

"Well…"

"Oh, I see." I chuckled. "Things haven't changed much since you left." She wasn't amused, so I hurried on. "Your idea of Easter hasn't moved beyond Good Friday. You should really be worried if he had told you you smell like Good Friday with the stench of crucifixion death wafting down from Golgotha." Afraid I was about to launch into another sermon for which I lacked the energy, I paused to catch my breath.

"So when he said I smelled like Easter, you don't think he was smelling death?" she replied a little more hopefully.

"Now you're catching on," I said. "Listen. Easter is about life, now and forever. Resurrection life now and for all eternity. The cross was empty on Easter morning. Jesus broke the chains of sin and death. Resurrection power has been loosed into the world and into our lives."

"So you think I'm safe?" she said.

"We should all be so safe," I said. "Smelling like Easter is a great thing. Something wonderful may be about to happen in your life."

She still sounded a little skeptical, but I knew from experience that sometimes it can take years for a sermon to sink in. "Sorry to bother you so late. I just didn't know what to make of it."

"You know what I hope?" I continued. Sometimes it's difficult to know when to conclude a sermon even when you're tired and the people are tired. "I hope you'll still smell like Easter on Monday morning. Then you'll really have something."

I wasn't sure she knew what to make of it all, but I felt it was time to conclude our conversation. "Sorry I didn't have my leaf blower going," I said with a short laugh.

"What?" she replied.

"Oh, nothing," I said. "Just remembering some of our previous conversations."

"Well, thanks for listening."

"Good to hear from you," I said as I returned the phone to its cradle.

But the conversation was continuing in my mind. In fact, my friend had raised a question I wrestled with long after I had gone to bed: "I wonder what I'll smell like tomorrow?"

Monday is a hard day to smell like Easter. And all the other days on the way to Mullinix. But I guess when a step here and there—or an action or a word—gives off even the slightest aroma of the presence of the resurrected Christ, my destination of achieving an elevated discipleship remains a real possibility.

A Good Day?

The physician turned to the priest and said bitterly, "I hate pain." The priest did not reply, as it was evident the doctor had more on his mind. "That's why I don't believe in God. How could there be a God with so much pain in the world?"

I had followed the doctor and the priest into the hospital elevator on the way to visit a parishioner on the fifth floor. Unfortunately, it was a fast elevator, so I missed most of their conversation. But it's a conversation that has been going on for centuries, and it would be too optimistic to believe it could have been solved between the first and fifth floor in a hospital elevator.

In fact, in my mind, the problem of evil, even with the best of answers from the smartest people, will continue to be a mystery beyond all our best explanations.

This does not mean, however, that questions are the only responses we can make to pain and suffering. I have seen remarkable responses that have carried individuals beyond the hopeless, helpless valley of unimaginable pain.

When I finally found my parishioner's room and we had talked for a while, I noticed an elderly African-American man in the first bed of this semiprivate room. He was an affable gentleman, and we began talking about his recent surgery and his hopes of going home that day.

Swinging his gangly legs over the side of the bed, he looked at me out of keen, warm eyes set in a face of deep wrinkles, the fruit of both age and hard living, and said in a pleasingly low, gravelly voice, "Live by m'self. Wife died las' year, and Doc said he couldn't turn m'loose 'til he's shore I can take care of m'self." Chuckling, he added, "Doc thinks I'm old. But what does he know? He's looking at th' paper and not at me."

He was still chuckling when his young doctor walked in. After exchanging pleasantries with us, the physician turned to his patient and immediately began testing his mental acuity. "Now if you had six apples and I gave you three more, how many would you have?"

The old man thought for a brief moment, and I saw his fingers moving where they lay on the white sheet. He chuckled again and replied, "I reckon I'd have nine o' them apples. But ya know what, Doc?" The young doctor shook his head. "You'd have three less. Prob'ly just barely 'nough t' make a decent pie," and he laughed at his cleverness. He was eager to get out of here.

The doctor smiled indulgently as he continued his examination. "Now, can you say, 'It's a nice day out today'"? The old man frowned, the wrinkles on his forehead growing even deeper. I was silently encouraging him. "Come on, man," I was thinking. "You can do that. You've been carrying on a fluent conversation for several minutes. That should be easy for you to say."

But my new friend shook his head and said sadly, "No sir, Doc, I don' think I c'n say that."

Puzzled, the doctor asked, "Why can't you say, 'It's a nice day out today'"?

"Doc, I cain't say that," the old man replied impatiently, "'cause I ain't been outside in four 'r five days now. I don' know what it's like out there."

Startled, the doctor took an involuntary step backward and then burst into laughter along with the rest of us. "You're ready to go home," the doctor said as he stood up to leave.

I've thought of that old man many times over the years, especially when I encounter pain and grief. Here was an individual who refused to take anyone else's word for reality. He insisted on speaking from his own experience.

That's the only satisfactory answer I've found for pain and grief. Even the best-reasoned arguments for the presence of evil in a world in which I also believe there is a good God in charge are not sufficient to meet our needs.

A man who had lost his wife in a car accident was left to raise two small sons alone. Through his anguish and tears he told me. "This is really, really hard to accept. I can't understand it at all." He paused and shook his head before continuing, "But I believe if I don't quit, God will give me strength and work it out."

He wasn't trusting an argument. He was trusting his personal, firsthand knowledge of a loving God to carry him through and bring something positive out of it. Reality was not what someone told him it was. Reality was personally experienced when the light of God's love kept breaking into the darkness of his deep grief each day.

In John's great vision of resurrection, he saw the suffering people of the world lined up before the throne of heaven. Of the risen Christ, John writes, "He will lead them to springs of living water. And God will wipe away every tear from their eyes" (Rev 7:17).

John's vision, of course, has to do with the kingdom to come. But if that kingdom has drawn near in Jesus in our present world, can we not experience that same God dealing with our suffering on this day?

When that experience becomes a personal reality along the way to Mullinix, that answer to my pain is sufficient to keep me loyal in the apprenticeship to the Christ I have chosen to live out.

Now that is a "good day."

Daffodils and Discipleship

I was startled out of my reverie when the young man leaped out of the car next to me at the intersection of Ironbound Road and Monticello Avenue near the College of William and Mary in Williamsburg, Virginia. It was one of those cool days just prior to the official beginning of spring, and my thoughts were on sunshine and warmer days ahead after a dark, cold winter.

I was in the right lane of three lanes when a young couple pulled up beside me to my left in the center lane. We had all stopped for the red light when the young man in his early 20s jerked open the passenger side front door and raced around the back of the car. Sprinting across the lane of traffic on his left, the somewhat desperate-looking young man stopped in the middle of a thick bed of daffodils at the height of their blooming glory.

Quickly picking a white daffodil and then two yellow ones, he ran back to the waiting car, where his female companion had been squirming anxiously in the driver's seat, fearful the light might turn green before her friend returned.

Plopping dramatically into his seat while slamming the door, the young man leaned toward the pretty driver, holding out the freshly picked bouquet with a smile and an exaggerated flourish. The young woman looked confused, as if she didn't know whether to smile or be angry. The anger side must have won because when the light turned green, she sped off a little faster than necessary, her tires squealing.

I could imagine the conversation as he presented the flowers to his sweetheart: "See, honey, I didn't forget your birthday!" Her response clearly demonstrated what the young woman thought of the degree of sacrifice involved in this spontaneous act of love.

As I pulled off, much slower than the young woman, I thought how unsatisfactory the man's efforts to correct his thoughtlessness must have appeared to his beloved. I've learned from personal experience that shortcuts in such things just don't get the job done.

That also seems to be true in our attempts to follow the Christ. In the middle of our crowded three-lane lives, we pause a moment now and then to pick a couple discipleship flowers, expecting them to blossom into a beautiful bouquet of spiritual transformation.

Paul shakes his head and says, "Continue to work out your own salvation with fear and trembling" (Phil 2:12).

The way to Mullinix is not an easy road. The transformation of folks like us into the character of Christ comes with great effort. "Fear and trembling" work is required.

Shortcuts are not an option.

Is God Ever Too Busy?

O n the second afternoon of the revival, Bert Browning said, "I want you to meet someone."

Bert and his wife, Rose, had been important parts of our church in its early years while they were students at the College of William and Mary. Bert later attended seminary and became a gifted preacher and pastor. He had invited me to be the guest preacher in a revival at one of his first churches.

When Bert parked his car at the end of a dead-end dirt road, no house was visible. "The road doesn't go all the way to the house, but it's just a short walk through these woods," Bert explained as we exited the car, which we had just noticed was low on gas.

Later, on the way to the 7:30 service, we ran out of gas and finally made it at 7:35, much to the relief of Rose, who had been busily rehearsing the emergency sermon all pastors' wives secretly carry in their purses.

Bert and I emerged from a sparse grove of small poplar trees to stand before an attractive squat cottage similar to the one my childhood imagination had pictured to be Old Mother Hubbard's abode. When a little dumpling of a smiling woman answered the door and invited us in while patting her gray hair fixed neatly in a bun on the top of a nodding, tiny head, I was certain I had stepped into a story-book world.

"Y'all come on in and have a seat," she said cheerfully, her chubby hands smoothing the wrinkles from a bright yellow-flowered apron covering three-fourths of a homemade dress. Her long dress almost touched the top of soft, black leather front-laced high-top shoes.

Now there was no doubt in my mind that my childhood dream of meeting some of my favorite Mother Goose characters had finally come true.

At any moment I expected a hungry little black and white spotted dog to come running into the tiny screened-in front porch where our hostess had invited us to sit in two white rattan rockers adorned with colorful homemade cushions. Instead of a little dog, however, through the open door leading into a smaller room, I saw an elderly man hunched over so severely that his chin almost touched his knees as his bony hands rested limply on the arms of a locked wheelchair.

Our hostess took her place across from us in a cane-bottomed, straight-back wooden chair. Settling in comfortably, she dumped a mess of butterbeans from a white pail bucket into her expansive apron lap and skillfully began shelling the lime-green butterbeans into a medium-sized sauce pan. Her small head nodded enthusiastically as Bert began telling their story.

"They don't have any children," Bert began.

I interrupted hopefully, "What about a little black and white dog?"

"No pets," Bert replied, ending the possibility that I was in the presence of Old Mother Hubbard, who had gone to the cupboard for food and found it bare so the little dog had none. Bert's voice jolted me back to reality. "But with no children or close relatives, she has to care for her invalid husband alone."

Since I can no longer call her by her fairy tale name, I'll call her Nell.

Bert then went on to tell how the church helped them all they could, but the hard work of tending to her husband's daily needs fell on the shoulders of his wife. "In spite of that," Bert continued, "Nell is one of the most cheerful persons I've ever met."

Nell kept glancing in my direction and smiling without missing a beat of her butterbean shelling. Finally, at a break in Bert's story, she said in a jovial voice, "I 'preciate all the Lord does for me. He takes care of me, and I thank 'im every day."

She paused and looked down at the half-full pan of shelled beans before continuing, "But he doesn't answer all my prayers." There was no hint of bitterness or resentment in her voice. She was simply stating what to her was an obvious fact.

We waited in respectful silence as Nell chuckled softly and said, "I don't mind, though. I know he's awful busy with all the folks that mus' be praying to 'im all over the world for all kinds of favors."

She looked down again and shook her head sympathetically as if she complete-ly understood and identified with the "Good Lord's" predicament. Sometimes life just becomes too heavy and too busy. "He's got so much on 'im, he cain't get around to ever' little thing we need. But I sure 'preciate all he does for me t' keep me goin'."

Bert and I glanced at each other with the silent understanding that this was no time to talk about an omniscient, omnipotent, omnipresent God who counts the very hairs of our head and cares about even the little things that concern us. All our attempts at theological explanations would not add one dot or tittle to this woman's intimate experience with and assurance of a God who enabled her to meet each day with endurance, courage, and good cheer.

Looking back these many years later, I am even more convinced that those like Nell who have known such an intimate relationship with the Christ are the ones who have added most to my own understanding of God. Our reasoned arguments over the "why" of God's actions are perhaps helpful at times, but Bert and I knew that on this day we were the students and Nell was the teacher. We were in the presence of someone who knew what it means to accept the vagaries of life in the assurance that there is a friend who walks with her.

Along the way I've encountered far too many people who possess a lot of theories and opinions about God but have never known him intimately as a daily companion. In my mind those folks are disqualified to speak knowledgeably about God. True knowledge of God appears to come mostly through relationship.

I left that little cottage that afternoon knowing this courageous woman had helped me understand more fully what Job meant when he cried out, "My ears had heard of you, but now my eyes have seen you" (Job 42:5).

At those special times when I am also able to speak of God in the same intimate language as Nell, I feel myself drawing nearer to Mullinix, my ultimate destination of being as fully possessed by the Christ as my stubborn resistance and other finite human frailties will allow.

Like Nell, I "'preciate" those sacred times when I did not settle for merely hearing about God but instead entered that holy place of "seeing" him.

In fact, that's probably what life in Mullinix is all about.

The Master or the Masters?

He walked through the center double doors with his foldup golf chair emblazoned with a large "Masters" logo under one arm and his "Augusta National" cap perched cockily on his head. Smiling broadly at the friendly greeter, he asked, "Now where do I go?"

There are times and places in life when we desperately need a guide. Walking into the Masters golf tournament on April 6, 2016, we quickly realized this was one of those times.

My two sons, Chris and Brian, and my nine-year-grandson, Brent, and I were gifted by a close friend of our daughter's with tickets for the day. We felt extremely fortunate since I had heard that tickets to the Masters were among the hardest tickets to come by for any sports event.

Our expectations were high as we walked through the tight security of the front gate, where I was detained for extra scrutiny since I had on a jacket with many pockets, (I've always liked pockets) containing two kinds of sunscreen, aloe for sunburn, and other assorted items for the long day, in addition to a belt with a brass buckle and a number of keys on a large keychain. Not only did the woman use her hand-held detector to scan my entire body several times, but she also made me walk through the screening door three times before she was satisfied.

My two sons and grandson, who had passed easily through security several minutes earlier, were laughing as they watched my dilemma from the other side of the checkpoint. When I was finally permitted to walk through the gate, the blue-uniformed officer continued to stare at me with suspicion.

The whole episode caused me to rethink my long-held belief that I had a face that inspired immediate trust, a face that made people so comfortable that they spilled their deepest-held secrets during our first counseling session. I even entertained the unsettling notion that maybe the passing years had brought a few hard lines along with the inevitable wrinkles.

All such reflections were quickly dispelled, however, as we were suddenly struck by the vastness, the beauty, and the palpable tradition of the Augusta

National Golf Course. "We need a tour guide," my older son, Chris, said, giving voice to our mutual feeling of being overwhelmed.

Strategically placed signs along several paths helped, but decisions about where to go—and when—in order to catch the best action remained. Occasionally, we would hear a tremendous roar and realize we had once again missed something big. Timing is everything.

For a while we wandered around aimlessly, taking in the beauty of the well-manicured course, stopping to sit in a grandstand and watch two pairs of golfers play through at one point, and then checking out "Amen Corner" until we finally found an advantageous spot from which to view the action on the seventh green. Standing next to the crowd-control rope—there were no grandstands here—we could see the golfers up close and wonder at how much smaller and average they appeared than when we watched them on television.

During a break in the action, I reflected on how much more accurate our assessment of people would be if we possessed the proper proximity from which to view them. Or maybe such stark reality would be more than we could handle. How much fantasy do we need to accept all the imperfections in ourselves and others? It's much easier to remain content with our false evaluations than confront the truth that sometimes requires large doses of grace.

An obviously agitated man walked into my study one morning and asked, "Can I be brutally honest with you?"

Forcing a smile, I replied, "Honesty is brutal enough. Put as much grace into it as you can."

Even though we were occasionally disillusioned by the appearance and performance of the golfers, it is always exciting to watch those who are working hard to be the best in any field of endeavor. Perfection in a broken world is unrealistic, but seeing folks determinedly strive to reach that goal gives hope to those of us who live farther from the ideal than we would like.

Rory McIlroy is my grandson's favorite golfer, and it was a real treat when Rory approached the seventh green paired with Jordan Spieth. The crowd-control security officer was very kind and made room for Brent to stand as close as possible to the players, saying, "Two of the best golfers in the world are coming through. You don't want to miss this."

As if to affirm my reflections on the difficulty of perfection, however, Rory and Jordan both bogeyed the hole. Then to emphasize our human frailty, a rather large man off to my right collapsed and fell backward. Fortunately, the crowd had deepened in anticipation of the appearance of Rory and Jordan, so the gentleman's fall was broken by a many-layered human cushion.

Shakily, the man told us it wasn't a heart attack but a low blood sugar problem. A young man standing next to me from Peoria, Illinois, fished a couple cookies from his jacket pocket, and after quickly consuming them, the fallen man was soon back on his feet, his blood sugar restored to an acceptable level.

My pastor mind, which has developed the disquieting, if helpful habit of seeing sermons as I walk along, reflected briefly on how wonderful it would be if two cookies could solve all the maladies of the human spirit as well as a low-glucose body.

Maybe one of our problems is that we like to think the solution to our brokenness can be simple and easy when what is required is a fundamental, dramatic transformation at the core of our being. A sermon title popped into my mind: "Are Two Oatmeal Cookies Really Enough?"

"Come on, man," I chided myself, forcing my eyes down the fairway as two more golfers approached the green. "You're supposed to be relaxing at a once-in-a-lifetime golf tournament." Just one of the hazards of having to come up with challenging, moving sermons every week for 45 years, I suppose.

Thirty minutes later, my back began aching terribly just beneath my right shoulder blade, where a weak spot remained from a severe bout with pleurisy when I was in middle school. I leaned over in an effort to relieve the stress and the pain.

That innocent movement caused a frenzied stir from those nearby, thinking I was about to emulate our fallen companion. When I explained that it was just an aching back, the young man from Peoria said with evident relief, "Thank goodness. I'm all out of cookies."

It was a good day with family and kind people and accomplished golfers and a beautiful golf course. The seven-hour trip from Williamsburg, Virginia, had certainly been worth it.

But the next day as we were returning home, our son-in-law, Steve, pastor of a large contemporary church in North Augusta, South Carolina, just across the Savannah River from Augusta, called to tell us about an interesting incident that had occurred in the second worship service of the day. We had attended the first one at 9:30 that morning before heading home.

The church building, a rather modern structure, sits just off Interstate 20, which leads into Augusta. A sign at the North Augusta exit, however, told motorists that exit 1 was an option for Masters traffic. If you moved over to the right lane immediately after exiting, however, you had no choice but to proceed into the church parking lot.

Which is exactly what the man I mentioned earlier did.

After finding a parking space, the excited man walked into the front foyer of the church with his chair and Masters cap, asking excitedly, "Now where do I go?"

Does it amaze you that anyone can be so unaware of his surroundings that he would mistake a church for the entrance to a golf course? One explanation could be that this particular man had spent every Sunday morning of his adult life on the golf course. ("Pastor, I can worship God on a golf course as well as I can in church.") Maybe that had happened so regularly that he could no longer tell the difference between the house of the Master and the home of the Masters.

I've seen it happen.

The more likely explanation, however, is that the majority of us follow signs blindly, trusting them to guide us to our destination, without applying any thought or logic or discernment along the way, barely noticing what we are passing or what is happening around us. GPS technology has contributed to this dilemma, I suppose.

Jesus talked much about staying awake because the kingdom was coming in him: "Jesus came to Galilee, proclaiming the good news of God, and saying, 'The time is fulfilled, and the kingdom of God has come near; repent, and believe in the good news'" (Mark 1:14–15).

Following that pronouncement, in all his words and actions, Jesus showed us what the kingdom of God looked like: humble service, forgiving love, sacrifice, generosity, and on and on Jesus kept erecting signs that we can follow if we want to become authentic citizens of his kingdom.

I don't know if that man who ended up in our son-in-law's church ever found the real Masters golf tournament. I would like to think that maybe he saw his mistake as a sign that he needed to pay more attention to the signs that lead to an eternal destination rather than a weekend stopover.

Occasionally, I've also seen such transformative thinking take place.

At least all this reminded me to be more intentional along my sometimes half-awake journey to Mullinix. If I'm ever to reach that place where I speak and act like Jesus, I must be alert not to misread the signs or ignore them completely and waste valuable time and energy finding my way back.

Robbing Us of Our "Insanity"

"This here the church where I c'n find an AA meeting?" The question came from a lanky middle-aged man with rheumy eyes looking at me plaintively from beneath a tattered John Deere cap pulled low in a vain attempt to hide his ravaged face.

A few moments before, I had pulled into the front parking lot of Walnut Hills Baptist Church, where I served as pastor for 35 years. The only other vehicle in sight was an old pickup parked on the Jamestown Road side of the parking lot, facing the busy parade of tourists heading toward the first permanent English settlement in the New World, just five miles west of our church.

This location, with Colonial Williamsburg and the College of William and Mary slightly over a mile to the east, meant that between the college students and tourists, we had new faces in our congregation every Sunday. That no doubt helped us ward off stagnation. But it also meant I encountered a myriad of doctrines and perspectives on Christianity that led to many challenging dialogues following our worship services.

Since people can become pretty passionate about their faith, or at least their long-held beliefs about their faith, some of these conversations leaned more toward monologues and lectures, leaving me very little opportunity to respond. A few of these folks accosted me at the door. Others waited and found me in my study in a back hall.

But most of our visitors were pleasant and interesting and asked insightful questions, which I welcomed. Their presence greatly enriched our worship experiences.

So I was not surprised to see a stranger climb out of what was once a red Ford pickup but was now liberally sprinkled with a wide assortment of rust spots. The tall but stooped man who slowly exited the driver's side was dressed in a long-sleeved flannel shirt and well-worn soiled jeans. His outfit, along with his overall demeanor, told a story of bad choices and bad luck, which are often close companions.

Thus, I had already anticipated his first words: "This here the church where I c'n find an AA meeting?"

"There is a meeting here today," I replied, reaching out to shake his slightly trembling hand. "But this one is for women." His face fell, so I hastily added, "I think the one you're looking for is about half a mile toward town at the United Methodist Church. It'll be on your right."

A strained smile, evidently unfamiliar to his pale, unshaven face, greeted my information. "Thank ya for that," he said, moving back toward his truck.

Then, hesitating, he looked at me with those sad eyes, which had obviously known their share of hopelessness, and said, "Just cain't seem to give these up." He nodded toward the cigarette held carelessly in his right hand. "Know they'll probably kill me some day, but somethin's gonna git us all, ain't it?" A strangled chuckle escaped his chapped lips.

"You're right there," I replied. "But I hope it's a while for both of us." He lowered his head and shook it in such a way that I wondered if he shared my optimism or my desire for a long life.

"I know cigarettes is bad," he continued. "But not bad as that air alc'hol." Shaking his head more furiously, he spat out, "That alc'hol will rob ya of yer insanity!"

This was no time to tell him he had meant to say "sanity" rather than "insanity," so I agreed with him and wished him God's blessings.

"Come back if you have trouble finding the church," I said, "but I don't think you will. It will be on your right facing Jamestown Road across from the college campus."

With a wave of his right hand, still holding the cigarette in his nicotine-stained fingers, he climbed into his truck and slammed the creaking door as I turned toward the front door of the church.

I was smiling over his use of the word "insanity" when a sudden thought stopped me in my tracks. "Wait a minute!" I said. If anyone in the hallway heard, they paid no attention. They were accustomed to their pastor having private conversations with himself. "He was right. That's just what we need. To be robbed of our insanity!"

A list of insanities began to parade through my suddenly energized mind. My brain never seems to function as well in the afternoon, but this encounter had awakened it from its after-lunch hibernation.

I thought about how we insanely insist on going our own way instead of following God's way. Or the insanity of trying to be Christian without also being a disciple. In some of our in-reach meetings, we would often speak of those "fringe" members who show up on Easter and Christmas. But I wonder if there are not many more "fringe" members who show up every Sunday but never make the critical decision to be an authentic disciple.

In a book I had recently read by Dallas Willard, The Great Omission, I recalled how Willard expressed the belief that the large majority of church members have made many decisions concerning their faith, but have never decided to become real disciples, real students, real followers.

Jesus made it clear how critical and how radical that decision is when he said, "Whoever finds his life will lose it, and whoever loses his life for my sake will find it" (Matt 10:39).

We need to be robbed of the insanity of choosing to be Christian and a church member and even being baptized without also deciding to submit our life to the continuing transformation required in becoming a recognizable follower of Jesus Christ.

I turned and rushed back through the church door to wave a "thank you" to the stranger for words I knew I would hold close for years to come in my quest for Mullinix, that place of authentic discipleship. But I saw that he had already exited the parking lot and was headed down Jamestown Road toward the help he was seeking for a powerful addiction.

I prayed that he would find it and lose his own insanity.

Following that encounter, I also learned to pray for myself, "Lord, this day, rob me of the insanity of seeking my destination of authentic discipleship through any means other than losing my life to find it."

Seven Miles from Home

My prayer was the most common of prayers: "Help!"

We were attempting to cross an already challenging span of the West Virginia mountains when the journey was made even more precarious by a sudden blinding blizzard. At least 98 percent of the interstate disappeared in a swirling whiteout.

Although I was certain he understood my cry for help, in my panic I fleshed out my desperate prayer for divine intervention. "Lord Jesus, please get us off this road safely. We will gladly sleep on a thin layer of decaying hay spread over a bed of fresh cow dung in a cold, isolated barn and call it blessed."

I knew the Lord had better accommodations at his disposal, but this was no time to be greedy.

I was leading our little caravan in a powerful F-150 Ford pickup pulling the largest U-Haul trailer I could locate in our hometown of Williamsburg, Virginia. We were on the way to relocate our younger son, Brian, and his wife to Cumberland College in Williamsburg, Kentucky. Immediately behind me were Brian, in his fully loaded car, followed by our wives in the third car, also fully loaded (the car, not our wives).

In our present blinded condition I was keenly aware that the only thing they were following were the taillights on my U-Haul trailer and that where I went they were going to go even if it meant certain death at the bottom of one of the deep ravines on both sides of the road. This was before the age of cellphones, and they had no idea that I was guessing at the road's location.

Squinting desperately through the hypnotic, dancing snow, I searched for a road sign that would assure me there was pavement somewhere beneath my truck tires now making uncertain paths through the soft snow.

"Lord," my prayer continued, "I haven't asked you for many signs through the years. Always felt asking for signs demonstrated a lack of faith. But please give me one now. Any kind of sign."

About a half mile farther down the white canvas of an interstate, my heart leaped as I made out the faint outline of what looked like an exit sign.

Going to Mullinix

"Please let this not be a mirage," I begged. "But if it is, or if it is real and I miss maneuvering onto the ramp, receive me and all those who will plunge into the ravine behind me into your eternal kingdom."

Descending the potential ramp at a crawl, a spontaneous "Hallelujah!" erupted from my tremulous lips as I spotted lights from a gas station penetrating the swirling snow just to the right of where the ramp ended. Feeling blessed far beyond what I deserved, I next saw rising over the top of the station an Econo Lodge sign.

I don't know why in that moment I thought of the visiting evangelist of my boyhood who objected vociferously to the old gospel song imploring the Lord to "build me just a cabin in the corner of glory land." If I remember correctly, he objected to that song on the theological grounds that there were only mansions and no cabins in heaven.

That evangelist had never been lost in a blinding snowstorm on an invisible highway in the winding mountains of West Virginia. The quality of the accommodations is of little concern when you are saved from that which threatens to destroy you. That little Econo Lodge looked like heaven.

After tightly hugging each other as only those can who have survived a battle together, we gratefully climbed out of our vehicles, gassed up our vehicles, and precariously continued our trek, slipping and sliding up the winding, ice-covered driveway to the little motel on top of a hill behind the gas station.

We made quite a racket stomping our feet to clear away the ice and snow before entering the warm, well-lit registration office of the Econo Lodge. It felt like home.

Well, not quite like home according to the elderly couple who walked in just ahead of us. Turning to us with a friendly smile and nodding toward his equally friendly wife, the old man said, "Bad storm, ain't it?"

"You can say that again," I replied enthusiastically, if not very eloquently.

Chuckling softly, the old man continued, "My wife and I live just seven miles up the road, but we cain't make it all the way home."

"Just seven miles?" I exclaimed.

"Yeah," his wife joined in. "Live on a little farm just seven miles up the road. But we're 'fraid we cain't reach it through this storm."

Nodding my head in vigorous agreement, I said, "I can certainly understand your dilemma. I feel terribly lucky to have made it to this Econo Lodge." Smiling, the elderly couple turned to register just ahead of us.

Later, snuggled comfortably in a warm, soft bed, I closed my tired eyes and poured out a heartfelt prayer of gratitude for family and exit signs and Econo Lodges and gas stations.

However, sleep didn't come for a long time as the old mountain man's words kept teasing my adrenalin-infused mind: "Seven miles from home but can't make it all the way."

Instead of sheep, I found myself counting people from years past who seemed to have come so close but never quite made it all the way home. Some were like King Agrippa, who appeared to want to believe Paul's words concerning the Christ but was unable to overcome his doubts and take that final step toward home (Acts 26:28).

I remembered others who had come through such horrendous storms that they were blind to the possibility of the existence of a loving God. Still others were reluctant to "think about anything that seriously" and were content to remain on the outer edge of discipleship, close enough to taste faith but never quite taking a healthy bite of it.

As I finally drifted off, I prayed for all those caught in fierce storms that somewhere up ahead they might find an exit and complete the trip home to safety.

And I prayed for myself that nothing would so blind me to the signs of God's presence along the way to Mullinix that I would stop seven miles short of being fully permeated and possessed by the Christ.

The old mountain man had smiled when he said it, but the sadness of the words still haunt me: "Seven miles from home but can't make it all the way."

Part Three

Curious Critters

Bully Fish Need Love Too

Our 6-year-old grandson, Brent, tenderly held the dead fish lying on a paper towel and looked up at me sadly, saying, "Papa, I just can't flush it."

That surprised me, because during the years we have shared the two aquariums located in our sunroom, Brent and I have witnessed the birth and death of many fish, and flushing a dead fish has never seemed to bother him. In fact, he has had a very healthy view of death as being a part of the normal cycle of life, saying to the dead fish as it swirled round and round in the toilet bowl, "See you later in heaven, fish. Go see your friends."

On this morning, however, he walked from room to room with the fish lying lifeless on the paper towel, reluctant to consign him to his watery grave. What made that even more surprising was that the white tetra, "Whitey," he held in both hands had bullied a number of other fish to death. Personally, I was glad to be rid of him.

"I guess I better not kiss him goodbye since he may have a disease," Brent said as he looked sadly at the drying, shriveling fish. Fifteen more minutes passed, and Brent was still restlessly roaming the house with the fish held carefully in front of him.

"Honey, isn't it about time to flush him?" I asked.

Looking down at the fish, Brent said sadly, "Papa, I can't."

"But you had no trouble with the others," I protested.

Shaking his head, Brent said, "But this one is a bully." After a brief pause he explained, "The devil is going to get him."

The fish Brent stubbornly held in his hands betrayed our trust again and again. We had moved him to a less crowded tank, thinking the increased space might lessen his aggression and help him reform. But he showed his lack of appreciation by bullying another fish to death. Whitey knew nothing about being a constructive member of fish society and needed to be incarcerated.

So we had restricted him to solitary confinement in a small net, where he died after two weeks. He was not a nice fish. He couldn't get along with any of his fish family, and we were angry with him on a daily basis. He was a hard fish to like.

And yet Brent was heartbroken over releasing him to what he interpreted as his eternal damnation.

"You know, honey," I said, trying to ease his agony, "God loves a lot more than we do."

"Even fish?" he asked hopefully.

"Well, the Bible says he watches over the birds of the air. Why not the fish in the water?"

As I watched a solitary tear slide down Brent's cheek, I felt a stab of judgment. How often have I wept over those who have never experienced the saving grace of our risen Lord? How long have I felt compelled to hold on to those wandering individuals, hesitating to move on and leave them to their fate?

Still concerned about "Whitey" but a little more hopeful, Brent finally realized there was nothing more left to do and watched sadly as the bully fish slid off the paper towel into the swirling water. We were both quiet for a while—he lost in his thoughts of the doomed fish and I still wondering if I had done enough to reach out to the bullies I have encountered along the way to Mullinix.

As we grabbed our tools to clean the aquariums for the remaining "good" fish, the words of Paul popped into my mind: "Let love be without dissimulation" (Rom 12:9).

That kind of love is hard, even toward fish, except in the tender heart of a six-year-old child whom Jesus said we must emulate if we are to inherit the kingdom.

Ducks Don't Notice the Unexpected

O ften, it's the unexpected that causes us to lose our way.

One year my father had about 30 ducks that populated his fish pond just down an incline to the left of the grape arbor with its heavy load of scuppernong and muscadine vines. The number of ducks at any particular time varied according to how many fell victim to predators creeping among them as they huddled on the banks during the night. A few of the baby ducks also became the unfortunate prey of large turtles grabbing their little legs as they floated peacefully across the water.

Even the most innocent of environments hold hidden dangers in this kind of world, I guess.

This year, Daddy had his largest flock ever. Each morning when he opened the storm door of the back porch leading to the carport and then out into the backyard, all 30 ducks would come rushing up the hill from the pond to meet him as soon as his feet hit the bottom step.

With heads held high in excited quacking, they would flock around his overalled legs and then make a sharp left turn toward the smokehouse, where my father kept their beloved shelled corn.

Oh, it was a sight to behold—30 fat, hungry ducks waddling eagerly behind my father, stumbling over each other in their efforts to be first in line for breakfast. Daddy looked as if he were walking on a rolling sea of white down.

On this day, however, as I watched the early morning ritual from the back porch window, my father deviated from his usual route and made a sharp right turn toward the garden instead of heading straight to the smokehouse.

I saw his change of direction clearly from my elevated vantage point, but all 30 ducks failed to notice and charged straight ahead toward their anticipated destination. Those hurrying, squawking ducks were almost to the smokehouse before they realized that "He Who Feeds" was no longer out front leading.

Have you ever seen a flock of 30 ducks have a panic attack? It was both hilarious and pathetic to watch 30 helpless ducks transformed from confident, loud quackers into questioning whiners, their yellow bills slowly opening, emitting uncertain sounds of lostness, their long necks stretching high, twisting from side to side in a desperate search for "He Who Feeds."

Two of the older, matronly-looking ducks, were standing nearer the grape arbor, a few feet to the left of the flock. Although I was watching through the glass-enclosed back porch about 30 yards away, it was easy to understand what they were saying. If you watch the expression in their eyes and read their body language, you don't have to be Dr. Dolittle to hear critters talk.

"Now, Gertrude, where did he go?"

"I don't know, Matilda," Gertrude replied.

Gertrude was easy to distinguish since a birth defect or a mauling at a young age caused her wing to hang out and down at an awkward angle. Her deformity was magnified by a distinctive limp resulting from a crooked leg.

"I don't know where he went," Gertrude repeated. "I was just following the tail feathers in front of me and never saw him take a different path. The possibility never even occurred to me that he might go a different way." Limping a couple steps farther from the flock, Gertrude confided sheepishly, "To tell you the truth, I never did get a good look at him, just following the flock like I always do."

"Well," Matilda replied, "I always try to follow Fred. He usually knows what he's doing, or acts like it at least. But I had trouble spotting him what with all this molting."

"I know what you mean. I haven't been able to tell the men from the women since we started molting. We all look alike. Well," Gertrude added, "everybody but me looks alike with this crazy wing and crooked leg."

"I hear that," Matilda replied. "Just yesterday I thought I was talking to Fred, and it turned out to be Emily."

"Emily's nice."

"Yeah, but I was telling a story I had heard about her," Matilda explained, drooping her head almost to the ground.

"How many times have I warned you about repeating stories, especially about those in our own flock?"

Gertrude shook her head in disgust as Matilda said contritely, "I just can't seem to keep a secret."

"That's why, even though you're my best friend, I don't tell you everything I hear—or think."

A brief silence hung over the two friends who had remained close for several years in spite of their differences. "I'm hungry!" Matilda suddenly quacked loudly. "Where did he go? Has he abandoned us?"

"Probably we abandoned him by not noticing where he was going," Gertrude concluded.

"This is embarrassing!" Matilda cried out again. "Look up there. Even Fred looks lost. Walking around in tight little circles right in front of everybody. Doesn't he care anything about appearances?"

"Appearances won't get us fed," Gertrude said.

"Well, what will?" Matilda's hunger was making her more and more impatient and cranky, like those cocky Canada geese who always felt their rights came ahead of the lowly ducks.

"Keeping a better watch on 'He Who Feeds' might do it," Gertrude replied.

"But he left us!" Matilda protested.

"No he didn't," Gertrude said. "We left him when we missed his unexpected turn." Matilda was looking at her friend doubtfully when Gertrude cried out, "Look! Here he comes now!"

Sure enough, out of the corner of my eye, I saw my father walking around the corner of the house from the garden headed toward the smokehouse.

Moving as fast as her disability would allow, Gertrude followed Matilda to gather with the flock around the dew-soaked bottom of the overalled legs of "He Who Feeds."

Hungrily, the ducks slurped up the grains of corn liberally tossed toward them by my father. "I know one thing," Matilda mumbled through a bill full of corn. "I'm going to follow a little closer and notice when 'He Who Feeds' takes an unexpected turn—even though I still think he ought to do things the same way every morning."

Gertrude only chuckled as she leisurely ate her share of the food. There was no hurry. Some was always left over.

I have always been intrigued with how Luke says Simon Peter and his partners in the fishing business, James and John, the sons of Zebedee, "pulled their boats up on shore, left everything, and followed [Jesus]" (Luke 5:11).

They left everything and followed Jesus, putting aside anything that might distract them from a single-minded, focused following.

But then after Jesus had been taken by the "chief priests, the officers of the temple guard, and the elders" (22:52), Luke says that "Peter followed at a distance" (22:54).

Unexpectedly, Jesus had willingly gone with those who came for him, while Peter wanted to fight. That was totally unexpected and more than Simon could accept. He hadn't seen Jesus' change of direction coming and was having difficulty adapting to it.

So now, "following from a distance," Simon Peter lost his connection and lost his way, denying three times that he even knew Jesus.

Thank you, you daffy ducks, for reminding me, on my way to Mullinix, that Jesus often makes unexpected turns, turns I completely miss if I am following at a distance.

Looking Back with Hands on the Plow

Ilooked around just in time to see the red mule on the outside tumble onto the little black mule pinned helplessly against the utility pole located at the left front corner of the field I was plowing. I froze in terror as I gazed down at the tangle of mules and harness and plow lines bound so tightly that only two legs out of eight were free to thrash aimlessly in a futile attempt to escape.

At the age of 10, I was barely tall enough to reach the plow handles when my father cut me loose to cultivate the gardens and corn fields located on both sides of our little cinderblock house squatting beneath huge oak and beech trees next to state road 731, two miles east of Mt. Gilead, North Carolina.

In addition to the field I was presently plowing, there was another similar-sized field to the left of the barn with one smaller field down a small incline below a hedgerow of honeysuckle and small saplings where we often grew cantaloupes and watermelons.

I plowed all these fields, but it was that front field next to the road, to the right of the house, that afforded me one of the most frightening experiences of my life.

Up until his death at the advanced age of 34, I plowed with "ol' Tom," a retired sawmill mule who had left most of his legendary strength in the wooded, rolling hills of the Piedmont region of North Carolina, where he had snaked huge logs to be transformed into usable boards at the sawmill.

But the primary reason "ol' Tom" looked so fragile could be attributed to the fact that he had left most of his teeth in anonymous corn cobs or they had simply fallen out along the way while he grazed on whatever was edible. So now he could only eat ground meal like an old man gumming soft food, making it impossible to keep his ribs covered with even a thin layer of flesh.

In today's world we probably would have been arrested for animal neglect. Some thought we should have been even back then.

One late afternoon, my Uncle Branson, one of Daddy's younger brothers, drove into our backyard where I was standing with Tom as he grazed on the thick grass (we seldom used a lawn mower with all the livestock around).

Uncle Branson jumped from his pickup, hollering at me with feigned alarm, "Jerry, where can I find a board real quick?"

Startled, I replied, "Down at the smokehouse in the shelter on the left, I guess. Why?"

"Need something to prop that mule up before he falls over," my uncle replied, doubling over in laughter.

Most of the time, I enjoyed my uncle's cleverness, but those words angered me. Tom and I were great friends, spending long, hot summer days in solitude as we plowed our small acreage. In all honesty Tom walked so slowly that if I could have found a way to fasten a book onto the plow handles, I could have done some good reading as he ambled along, barely moving until we turned at the end of the row and headed back toward the barn.

Why his speed increased so dramatically when he saw the barn was a mystery to me. Surely he couldn't have enjoyed his bland diet of ground meal that much. So I assumed Tom was just eager to return to his stall, get out of the hot August sun, and just rest. Well, he was retired and deserved it. So I never pushed him to go faster, just glanced over at the trees to my right once in a while to confirm that we were, in fact, still moving.

Those were good, solid, peaceful days of normality and the satisfaction of a job well done. But those days never last forever. Many years ago, one of my parishioners liked to say, "Jerry, everything has a shelf life." I learned that lesson quite young.

Things changed dramatically for me on the day I discovered Tom bicycling his legs against the ground in a desperate attempt to rise from his supine position behind the barn next to a small wooded area. He died there after an hour of suffering. But that's another story.

That was when my plowing experiences altered forever. One of our neighbors, Mr. Macy Haywood, a very distant relative, was kind enough to loan us two young, sleek, energetic mules who had just one gear—overdrive. With these two mules harnessed to the plow, I raced down the furrows, struggling to keep the point in the ground and maintain a straight line.

I must have been fairly successful in that straight line business because when Daddy walked out to the garden after work one afternoon, he looked up and down the rows and said, "Did you put down a string to guide you?" For a brief moment I thought I had done something wrong since my father never gave complete instructions, counting on us to fill in the blanks. Maybe I hadn't filled in the blanks correctly.

But then he continued, "I don't think I was ever able to plow a fur' as straight as that." You understand that in rural North Carolina we didn't have time to bother with final syllables, so it was always "fur'" instead of "furrow."

My father was an exceptionally kind man, but he never gave out compliments easily, for fear we might get the "big head," which for his generation was the eighth deadly sin.

Now, of course, "big head" was similar to "pride" but was considered a mutated first cousin, much more unseemly and showy than the more discreet sin of pride. "Pride" could be hidden. "Big head" insisted on pushing itself out front where everyone could see it on full display.

So my parents' generation did their best to keep us young'uns humble and thereby assuring us of a respectable place in the community and an eternal home in heaven. Funny how that never seemed to affect our self-esteem, which is such a great concern for parents today. Self-worth must be more complicated than merely giving out compliments.

On this day, however, my father had given me a compliment, and I swelled with pride or most likely, as later developments revealed, with that dreaded "big head." Regardless, I developed the almost unconscious habit of looking back at my straight furrow as I reached the end of each row. Now at the same time that I was looking back, I was also pulling the mules around for the return trip.

That seemingly innocent habit was the catalyst for the paralyzing scene that now lay thrashing before me on the freshly plowed red soil. Just as quickly, however, another horrific scene flashed into my mind.

I was standing before Mr. Macy with the two bridles from his mules in one hand and the remainder of the harness in the other. "Mr. Macy," I was stammering, "I'm so sorry, but I had to shoot both your mules."

Totally mystified, he was silently staring back at me, rapidly chewing the ever-present plug of tobacco in his left cheek. "Yes, sir," I was mumbling softly. "Had to shoot both of them. Broke their legs."

Finally finding his voice, Mr. Macy said incredulously, "Broke their legs? H-how in the world?"

Unable to look him in the eye, I whispered, "Plowing. Looking back."

That awful scene freed me from my paralysis, and I began loosening everything that was tied or clipped or knotted as fast as my trembling slender fingers could move. Fear does indeed increase one's strength, as I was able to loosen knots I never could have moved under normal circumstances.

After a few frantic minutes, which seemed like hours, the now-freed red mule on top simply slid off and stood up, followed quickly by the black mule that had been trapped on the bottom. Seemingly unperturbed, both of those tough old mules snorted to clear the dirt from their nostrils, shook the dust from their sweat-stained bodies, and waited calmly for me to hitch them back to the plow and continue the task at hand.

I turned my face toward the Carolina blue sky and shouted a prayer of thanksgiving for the durability and toughness of mules.

Many years later, when I came across Jesus' admonition that "no one who puts his hands to the plow and looking back is fit for service in the kingdom of God" (Luke 9:62), I didn't have to read it twice in order to understand what he meant—or the dangers involved in looking back.

Once we have started the joyful but often difficult, thorny journey of following Jesus, we must resist the temptation to look back and find excuses for stopping or taking a detour or even pausing in the journey. Or maybe like me at 10 years of age, developing a mild case of the "big head" and looking back in pride while congratulating myself on how straight I've been walking toward Mullinix.

Pride does indeed go before the fall. I have seen it with my own eyes in the fall of two innocent mules.

Does Jesus Care
about Harelip Puppies?

The Wednesday evening Bible study had ended, and I had opened the service for prayer requests. Most of them were quite heavy.

A man asked for prayer for a brother in the last stages of prostate cancer who was now under the care of hospice. Someone mentioned a woman in our church whose husband had died and requested help in taking food to the grieving family. This was serious stuff, and the challenges and pain of life were hanging over us like a heavy, dark cloud.

That was when a young man in his early to mid-20s sitting with his wife near the back of the sanctuary raised his hand to be recognized. "Our dog has just had a litter of puppies, and we would like to ask for prayer for finding them good homes," he intoned gravely.

An involuntary chuckle escaped the lips of a man sitting near the front, when suddenly he realized the young man was serious and tried quickly to convert his snicker into a cough. He wasn't very successful.

Unfortunately, the new puppy-daddy failed to notice and continued in that same serious tone, "We need special prayer for one of the puppies." Pausing for dramatic effect, he continued solemnly, "He has a harelip."

That was more than the three dozen or so folks gathered for the Wednesday evening Bible study/prayer service could handle. Kind as they were, they could no longer suppress their laughter, and an explosion of hilarity filled the sanctuary.

Trying hard to keep a straight face but afraid of also losing my composure if I repeated the request as I usually did, I kept watching the young man, who was now looking around totally confused, his face turning red as the laughter slowly subsided. I immediately closed the time for requests and began the prayer time.

I confess that I was unable to include the specially challenged puppy in my prayer.

Immediately following the service, I rushed toward the young man, apologizing for our insensitive, boorish behavior. With a sheepish smile he replied generously, "Well, thinking about it now, I guess it did sound kind of trivial in comparison to the problems other people were having." Then he frowned and added, "But didn't you say in your sermon a couple weeks ago that God is concerned about every little thing in our lives?"

I guess I'm still a little surprised when people take my sermons seriously enough to affect their worldview and even their lifestyle. Mostly, I tend to be pretty skeptical about the lasting effects of my preaching.

But I've always told my parishioners that the results of a sermon are 49 percent on me and 51 percent on them. When one man asked me why I place a higher burden on the congregation than on the preacher, I said, "Mostly for dramatic effect. Had a woman tell me one day that she worked so hard during the week, she couldn't wait to sit in church on Sunday morning and do nothing. Met lots of folks over the years with that attitude toward worship." Smiling at the man, a good friend, I said, "I know I'm going to work at it, but I'm not so sure about you."

Nodding my head in agreement with the young man's memories of my sermon, I said, "Well, since Jesus assures us that even the hairs of our head are numbered, seems reasonable to believe that everything that concerns us catches his eye." Matthew 10:30 had been my text for the sermon the young man remembered.

Through the years I've noticed that we most often speak of the great things God has done—and we should. However, I've also noticed that our daily lives most often have to do with small things. Small problems and small burdens nibble at us each day. Likewise, we are touched most often with small blessings and small miracles.

Children seem to be more aware of this than grownups. Our oldest granddaughter weighed 2 pounds, 6 ounces, when she was born prematurely. Family and close friends patrolled the hospital corridors in Evansville, Indiana, day and night, making many trips to the chapel during the three months she hovered between life and death in the neonatal ICU unit. We needn't have worried because God had something in mind for her.

Kayla is now a beautiful young woman who leads the children's ministry in the church where her father is pastor. She recently wrote this on their church's blog: "Working with children, I am able to experience a sweet perspective of God. When children pray, they tell God everything and ask for anything. Whether their dog has a boo-boo or the neighbors down the street lost their basketball and need a new one, nothing is too small for God to care about in their eyes."

When I read that, I began thinking about the day the disciples came to Jesus asking, "Who is greatest in the kingdom of heaven?" He did not answer their question directly. Instead, Jesus spoke first of the requirements for entering the kingdom: "Truly, I tell you, unless you change and become like children, you will never enter the kingdom of heaven" (Matt 18:3).

The key word here seems to be "change." We were all children once, but now Jesus says we must "change" to become children again. So something must have happened to us on the way to adulthood, something that wasn't good because it has the power to keep us out of the kingdom of heaven. Maybe it has something to do with the fact that young children have not yet been so shaped or misshaped by "cultural modifiers" that they are able to maintain their innate ability of viewing the world with untarnished eyes.

That makes me wonder if our laughter at that prayer meeting years ago contained more than a sense of triviality that harelip puppies were included in the same sentence with cancer. Was there an underlying discomfort of seeing child-likeness in a grownup?

And was that prayer service a microcosm of what we are doing all the time—training each other to change from childlikeness into, well, what? Do we mistakenly confuse childishness with childlikeness and therefore insist that we "grow up" until we have transformed our childlike trust into grownup sophistication and skepticism?

I still have trouble praying for a harelip puppy in public, although I have noticed that in my private prayers I include more and more little things that are of special concern to children.

More and more, I'm coming to realize that my journey toward Mullinix, toward becoming a full kingdom citizen, is a journey into childlikeness, into believing like a child that God just might care about harelip puppies—or at the very least care about those of us who care about harelip puppies.

The other night, growing agitated at the endless "adult" TV offerings, I caught myself surfing the channels for reruns of Mister Rogers' Neighborhood, a show that celebrated and nurtured children of all ages.

So maybe there's hope for me.

The Many Sides of a Canada Goose

It was one of those pastoral scenes I would like to have commissioned Norman Rockwell to paint and preserve for posterity.

Brent, the youngest of our grandsons, and Bella, one of our granddogs, and I were silently basking in the warmth of the sun as it caressed our backs during an early fall afternoon. Occasionally, our tranquility was interrupted as we pulled a wriggling largemouth bass or multicolored bream from the catch-and-release pond at Chickahominy River Park, two miles down John Tyler Highway from our home in James City County, Virginia.

We didn't mind the brief interruptions of catching fish, but we weren't at all prepared for the sudden, wild, raucous honking of two large Canada geese charging hard at us. Side by side, they raced toward our fishing spot on the west bank of the pond, tiptoeing across the surface of the water while stretching their huge wings to their maximum expansion of 6.1 feet in order to make themselves as large and intimidating as possible.

It was working. We were intimidated.

Normally, I love the honking of Canada geese. My wife and I live two blocks from the James River and often hear them flying over our house in their frequent travels to and from the river. The honking of these majestic birds is a pleasurable call to the freedom and wildness of the great outdoors, where I have always felt most at home.

When I learned from experts who claim to understand geese, that the honking represents words of encouragement to the goose who is taking his or her turn at the vortex of the v-formation, I enjoyed that honking even more. Can't help but wish the church could be more like that—if you're not leading the charge at that particular time, at least call out words of encouragement for the ones out front.

When Brent and I first saw the pair of geese now charging toward us, they were floating gracefully across our peaceful pond. I told my grandson they probably had a nest on the other side since the female only made brief excursions from the opposite thickly weeded east bank, where she always kept a watchful eye.

Love and peace reigned.

But now, startlingly, we were exposed to another side of the Canada goose. In fact, things were looking a little scary for our gang. Maybe Bella's presence triggered the protective instincts of these raging geese, but they needn't have worried. Big, bad Bella was crouching behind a green lawn chair, her tail tucked tightly between her legs.

Fortunately, these Canada geese were not French-Canadian and spoke fluent English because when they were a mere 50 feet from us, I called out in a loud voice, "Now hold on there! You don't want a piece of these three musketeers," which I said mostly to bring a smile to Brent's face, a face that had begun to show definite signs of high anxiety.

However, it also worked for the geese as they immediately drew in their massive wings, lowered themselves quietly into the water, made a lazy U-turn, and swam back toward the opposite bank. Peace was restored, and we went back to fishing for the next largemouth bass. Of course, the smallmouth bass were better jumpers and created more excitement, but we had had enough excitement for one day.

Unknown to us, however, there was more excitement to come during the next few days.

As the sun was setting on Friday evening of the following week, the mother goose was once again floating gracefully across the water, looking eagerly southwestward toward the mouth of the larger pond where it spilled into a sister pond.

"That's the direction from which her husband flies home about this time of day," I told Brent as we prepared to watch the joyful homecoming. It was obvious they were newlyweds since she was always happy to see him return home at the end of the day, rising out of the water to go meet him with a warm, welcoming kiss at her first glance of his topping the tall pines.

But we were surprised that on this day, almost as soon as the goose-wife had risen out of the water, she made a frantic U-turn, rushing back home, followed closely by a young gander much smaller than her husband. Brent and I looked at each other in bewilderment until we saw hubby come swiftly swooping in, almost touching the tail feathers of the young interloper.

We watched in amazement as with angry honks the jealous husband chased the handsome stranger across the pond directly in front of us, close enough for us to touch with a long cane fishing pole, until they both disappeared over the treetops to the north.

In a few moments the husband returned, but his anger had not subsided as he landed near his spouse, flapping his wings furiously, leaving no doubt about the level of his displeasure. Brent, Bella, and I watched in fascination as the young married couple engaged in a time-honored lovers' spate, perhaps the first for this pair. It was easy to follow their argument.

"Woman, what are you thinking, flirting with that young gander?"

"But, honey," his wife replied as she floated meekly up beside him. "I thought it was you and…"

Before she could continue, the enraged spouse honked, "Be serious, now! I make two of that scrawny bird!"

"No sweetheart, you make three of him, easy," his wife replied, reaching out to stroke him soothingly with her right wing.

"That's why I can't believe you got us confused. It was like you were expecting him!" the husband roared, watching her out of the corner of his eye while shaking his head so emphatically that his neck feathers fanned out in all directions.

"No, baby, I was waiting for you. The sun was just a little lower than usual and got in my eyes. You know the seasons are changing," his wife replied in that same subservient tone. "Besides," she said, "you were late," using the well-known method of deflection common in most such marital conflicts.

"Well, I guess I'll just have to buy you a pair of sunglasses," the male gander spat out sarcastically as he swam toward the middle of the pond, employing the sudden exit strategy popular with most members of the male species.

"Where're you going?" his worried wife called after him.

"Nowhere! Out!" her mate replied as he sank into a pouty silence.

"Remember," she yelled across the water. "You have to come back! Canada geese mate for life! Ask the park ranger!" Her husband didn't reply.

Brent and I and even Bella were totally exhausted from witnessing this scene. It was like being in the middle of an M-rated videogame—conflict and anger and war.

However, just two weeks later, we were surprised to see three little goslings floating peacefully behind their mother, whose calm demeanor had been completely restored. As the quartet drew closer and closer, Brent and I and even Bella remained still as we watched the mother lead her three small children onto our spot on the bank, walking slowly by our chairs, headed to the field behind us, where for the next few weeks she would teach the little ones to forage for food.

"Can you believe that's the same goose that just a couple weeks ago was charging at us, ready for battle?" I asked Brent. Brent smiled as he shook his head without replying. I continued, "But this, too, is what it means to be a Canada goose. We don't really know her unless we see all parts of her nature."

I wasn't sure he understood what I meant, but my mind had wandered to the woman many years back who told me she loved Jesus but was afraid of God. I tried to help her see that God was one and the Son and the Holy Spirit were simply different manifestations of God the Father, not three gods with three different natures.

I soon discovered that this devout woman had developed her understanding of God from some of the harsh stories of his anger and vengefulness in the Old Testament and never understood that the unconditional love revealed in his son was a much fuller story of God's nature.

It took me many years to notice something that I had always skimmed over in the "great commission": "All authority in heaven and earth has been given to me. Therefore, go and make disciples of all nations, baptizing them in the name of the Father and of the Son and of the Holy Spirit, and teaching them to obey everything I have commanded you" (Matt 28:18–20).

Now, of course, in all my baptisms through the years, I have used this Trinitarian formula ("I baptize you in the name of the Father, the Son, and the Holy Spirit"). But a thought came to me one day that I hope was from God and not my own fallible imagination (I often struggle to tell the difference between a word from God and a word from me).

Anyway, one day I began wondering if my formula for baptizing folks in the name of the Trinity also included the responsibility to teach the new convert the different sides we have experienced of God's nature. The last part of the great commission seems to give us the mandate to tell about the God who reveals himself as the Father who created all things; the Son, who came to earth to identify with us and die for us; and the Holy Spirit, who is God walking with us each day.

I've noticed that we also have trouble seeing the different sides of folks we meet. We experience one side of an individual or one characteristic and assume that's the sum total of whom he or she is. Without the benefit of any additional information or extending even a thimbleful of grace, we confidently compose their life's story, writing a conclusion we then refuse to question.

Guess that means if I am to grow into an authentic reflection of the Christ on the way to Mullinix, I had better be awake to the many-sided fullness of all of God's marvelous creation.

Funny what a goose can teach you.

Eagles Eat Roadkill Too

Sometimes disillusionment can ambush you around the next curve. It happened to me one sunny spring morning filled with the promise of good things to come.

I had just turned left onto Centerville Road off John Tyler Highway, a quarter of a mile from the entrance to our home in First Colony, when I passed a field on my right often filled with grazing deer. On this morning, however, one of the deer had grazed a little too near the road and lay at the edge of the field where a passing vehicle had unceremoniously dispatched her limp body.

But that wasn't what disturbed me since that was a common sight in an area overpopulated with deer who had been stripped of their natural habitat by overdevelopment. Nor did it bother me that the fallen deer was being consumed by a flock of dark-black turkey vultures, a necessary anti-littering process.

But the thing that caused me to swerve and almost wreck my 2001 Oldsmobile Aurora was two regal white heads rising above the sea of bobbing, ugly black heads. Startled, I realized they were bald eagles.

Bald eagles had long been my heroes. A large collection of eagles once filled my church office and now my home study. Pictures of majestic eagles flying undeterred through raging storms lined my walls, many of them gifts from parishioners.

When folks would question me about my seeming obsession with eagles, I would quote Isaiah 40:30: "Those who wait on the LORD shall renew their strength; they shall soar on wings like eagles."

For me, eagles represent the majesty of God and the ability of those who wait in trust on God to soar through the worst of storms.

Of course, I had read that hungry eagles sometimes resort to scavenging, seeking to satisfy their need for energy to support their massive wings as they seek the air currents high in the heavens. Even though their flight seems effortless, I know that like great athletes who make difficult plays seem easy, the flight of the bald eagle requires much stamina.

But I was hoping to avoid a scene like the one that unfolded before me in the bright morning light. The eagle's natural element is the air. Its feet are not designed for walking on the ground, with one toe pointing backward and three forward. Flying is the natural and only comfortable environment for the eagle.

So everything within me protested as I frantically searched for a way to redeem the sight of two majestic eagles feasting at a dead deer breakfast with nasty, blood-covered vultures whose very ugliness seemed fashioned for a life of scavenging.

So I wrote a sermon for that Sunday with the title "Even Eagles Eat Roadkill," a title so unsavory that my secretary walked into my office while working on the bulletin and asked if she were reading that correctly.

My intention was noble. I wanted badly to redeem the sight of eagles feasting alongside vultures at the roadside table. And the concept was theologically sound. We who were meant to soar with the eagles as overcoming conquerors in a fallen world sometimes forget to wait in trust on the Lord and find ourselves in the spiritual condition of eating roadkill.

But the execution of the sermon and the delivery were crippled by the despair of a heavy heart I could not quite overcome. The Sunday before, one of our church members had come up to me and said, "Jerry, I don't believe you have a bad sermon in you." This Sunday, a very perceptive and sensitive young woman remarked with a pained expression on her face, "Jerry, I think that's the worst sermon you have ever preached."

Humility is never a problem for a pastor. Someone is always happy to administer a heavy dose of stark reality, which often immediately follows on the heels of soaring compliments.

After over a quarter of a century, that experience of seeing majestic eagles eating roadkill, and my failed attempt to draw inspiration from it, still pierces my soul. But maybe that pain is the redemptive part of the whole sordid episode.

Somewhere in my readings through the years, I have heard Paul referred to as a "high-flying eagle," often soaring at an altitude not many of us have reached, in his understanding and experience of the risen Christ.

In fact, in his letter to the Corinthians, Paul talks about being caught up into paradise, so near he was to God. Oh, yes, soaring like an eagle, the majestic wings of his soul spread wide to catch the highest currents of the Spirit.

But then sometimes it seems Paul had to settle for roadkill: "There was given me a thorn in my flesh, a messenger of Satan, to torment me" (2 Cor 12:7–8). Paul begged for the thorn to be removed. He felt as if he could no longer bear the taste of roadkill.

God's answer, however, was not in cleaning up the roadkill and replacing it with an appetizing buffet, but in offering a heavy dose of grace: "My grace is sufficient for you" (12:9). And Paul, to his surprise, found it to be true. Through the experience of the pain, Paul was being made into a better person, if not a more comfortable person.

"To keep me from becoming conceited" (1:27), he said. The period of eating roadkill gave him power to soar to even greater altitudes of the Spirit, no longer tethered to earth by his misguided estimation of his own strength.

I need to remember on the way to Mullinix, when painful circumstances force me to feed on roadkill, that God can use that ugly experience as a doorway through which he gifts me with grace that can lift me to greater and greater heights until I am soaring again with the eagles.

Might not have been a good sermon, but it sure was a valuable lesson nudging me on toward Mullinix, the pinnacle of discipleship.

Locked In with Our Fears

My agile wife disappeared quickly around the corner of the darkened little wood-frame country store to vomit in private. Just as quickly, she reappeared and jumped into the front seat in a panic, slamming the door behind her, crying, "There's a Sherman Gepherd dog back there!"

The high school students in the back seat of our Mercury station wagon burst into uncontrollable laughter. It wasn't that they were insensitive to Jean's dilemma. In fact, they had taken turns experiencing that same gut-wrenching illness during the weeklong youth retreat at Eagle Eyrie, our Virginia Baptist state assembly grounds. But the hilarious scene overrode their empathy, and the raucous laughter continued for many more miles as I pulled out of the dirt parking lot and resumed our four-and-a-half-hour trip to our homes in Falls Church.

Strangely, that scare seemed to have cured Jean's nausea. I knew a sudden fright could cure hiccups, but it was good to know that it also worked with nausea. However, the experience did not cure Jean's lifelong fear of dogs.

When she was a young girl, a "Sherman Gepherd" had bitten her lower leg as she was walking alone to a friend's home and left her with an irrational fear of all dogs, no matter how harmless.

It was difficult to find a more harmless dog than Droopy, a short-legged black-and-brown-spotted little beagle that enjoyed a spoiled existence with my mother and father and younger sister, Donna, after all the older children had left home. Droopy's primary deficiency was his pathological need to be loved, exhibited by his demand for extravagant petting while sitting in a warm, welcoming lap.

Jean's lap was neither warm nor welcoming. Thus, it became an irresistible challenge for a desperately needy dog. From the time our family would arrive for a visit at my parents' home in North Carolina, Droopy would wait on the top step at the back door for Jean to appear, the signal for his writhing, full-body wag to begin. Instinctively, he knew that a little tail-wagging would not be sufficient to break through the wall of Jean's fear, so his entire body participated in extravagant wiggling.

This contest of wills would continue throughout our visit with Jean venturing outside only when accompanied by another adult strong enough to fend off Droopy's enthusiastic advances. His tenacity was a thing to be admired. Even though he made no progress in his attempts to be cuddled by this short, blonde woman who always seemed to be in a hurry, Droopy was not about to give up.

HIs stubbornness was demonstrated in dramatic fashion when it was time to begin our trip back to Williamsburg. Our three children and I loaded the car while Jean remained safely indoors, handing the suitcases through a crack in the back door. When everything had been packed, Jean took a deep breath and raced for the car with Droopy happily on the heels of his unrequited love.

Jerking open the rear door of the four-door Mercury station wagon, Jean jumped in, slammed the door, and quickly locked it. Safe at last.

But to her horror, when Jean turned to say goodbye to her in-laws, there sat Droopy on the seat beside her, his eyes filled with triumph and his long, wet tongue eagerly darting out to give her the kisses he had been emphatically denied over the past few days.

My mother had seen Droopy sneak into the back seat just before Jean slammed the door, and her laughter exploded into uncontrollable hilarity. Daddy reached over to steady her for fear mother might collapse onto the graveled driveway. From that day until her death in 2008, mother would repeat the story, between gasps of laughter, until it found a firm place in our collection of family lore.

After finally recovering from the shock of the unexpected interaction with Droopy, Jean laughed along with the rest of us as our children enjoyed taking turns telling the story for at least the first third of our trip home. Finally, exhausted from the telling and the laughing, our three children had fallen asleep, and all became quiet.

That was when I began to reflect on the ever-present phenomenon of fear and how we handle it. Many of us run from our fears and search for that place where we can shut the door, trapping our fears outside. Sadly, more often than not, we discover those fears have followed us into our supposedly safe place and taken a seat beside us, locked in by our own hand.

So I began to wonder if instead of vainly trying to shut the door on our fears, the secret might be to open the door to the perfect love of God. John wrote, "There is no fear in love. But perfect love drives out fear" (1 John 4:18).

Is it really possible that our insides can be so filled with God's love that there is no room for fear?

If I am ever to reach Mullinix, that place where I experience enough of God's love to rest from my fears, I guess I had better be careful what I shut out and what I let in.

Over the years Jean has opened our home to babysit all kinds of dogs for our children, even a huge, lovable Doberman Pinscher named Sam, who enjoyed ambling over to where she was sitting and resting his big head on her lap, daring Jean to bolt.

She never did.

Standing with the Goats

I was startled by the sudden cry from out of the darkness on my left. "Jeremiah! Jeremiah! Jeremiah!"

With eyes straining toward the outline of a faint shadow, I saw my father standing in the middle of the black asphalt, two-lane rural road with his face turned toward the starlit heavens. Daddy's voice was so imploring and plaintive that I hesitated to look up for fear the ancient prophet might actually poke his head from among the stars.

When Daddy built our home place in 1947, he plopped it down in the middle of five acres of thick kudzu where a home belonging to Mr. Franklin Haywood had recently burned to the ground. But the devastating fire had little effect on the kudzu. That's not surprising since very little has much effect on kudzu.

As I understand it, kudzu was brought to the United States in order to fight erosion. It certainly did that but also began fighting much more. Growing a foot each day and strong as a nylon rope, that persistent vine rapidly covered pastures and fields and even our yard as it crept irresistibly toward our newly constructed home.

I was personally acquainted with the satanic nature of this blight after trying to plow through it at 10 years of age with an elderly mule whom I have described in another story.

I was further handicapped by lacking knowledge of all the best cuss words at such a young age. Well, I was familiar with them from riding the school bus to Mt. Gilead School with some gifted profaners from Pekin, a crossroads community five miles to the east, but my mouth lacked the experience of making them recognizable to my plowing companion, who no doubt possessed a far more substantial vocabulary of cuss words than I from his days of snaking logs in a sawmill years ago.

However, in spite of my lack of practice, I manfully tried to call down God's wrath on that tool of Satan as best I could when the plow point would suddenly become hung in an unyielding vine almost jerking me face first onto the crossbar of the plow. Or when a knot of kudzu vines tossed the plow point out of the soil altogether.

Many years later, my younger brother, Kent, owned the property next door to my parents' five acres and thus inherited his share of kudzu, which rapidly began to overtake his pastureland. Kent never lacked for intelligence, so he had an idea about that kudzu. He bought three goats and named them Joshua, Jeremiah, and Jessie, since I'm sure he knew the coming battle would require help from God's chosen prophets. I thought that was a brilliant idea since a healthy goat can eat about eight pounds each day and goats consider everything they can get in their mouths a delicacy.

What Kent hadn't counted on, however, was that even a goat wants a varied diet on occasion, just as we humans. For instance, I love oysters: fried oysters, roasted oysters, oyster stew, oyster Rockefeller, and even an occasional raw oyster if it's accompanied by an abundance of saltine crackers and cocktail sauce.

When I was serving as an interim pastor at Saluda Baptist Church, located in Middlesex County, Virginia, a group of good church folk took me to a fundraiser at a firehouse in Waterview, a few miles north of Saluda on Route 17.

As we finally pushed back from the table, one of my church friends asked me how many oysters I estimated I had eaten. "Exactly three dozen," I replied quickly with a satisfied burp.

"You actually counted them?" he asked in astonishment.

"Have to," I said. "I don't want to overeat."

Recently, I returned to that church to preach when the new pastor was out of town. I asked when the next semiannual fundraiser was taking place. A friend replied somewhat sheepishly, "They told us not to tell you."

"What do you mean?" I asked, surprised and a little hurt by the comment.

"Well," my friend continued with an amused twinkle in his eye, "you know this is a volunteer fire department, and these oyster roasts are how they raise money to keep operating."

"I know all that," I replied. "What does that have to do with them not wanting me to know about the next fundraiser?"

"Well," he drawled, "the way it come t' me from the chief was, 'Y'all are welcome, but don't bring that preacher with you. The last time he was here, we lost money on 'im.'" My friend burst out laughing, but I knew there was a kernel of truth in his story.

My point is, I love oysters, but if I ate them for breakfast, lunch, and dinner, I would soon be craving a plate of spaghetti topped with three large, delicious homemade meatballs like the ones my daughter-in-law, Shelley, makes. Evidently, goats are no different, and soon Joshua, Jeremiah, and Jessie began breaking through the pasture fence in search of other foods to satisfy their voracious appetite.

So it was not unexpected that while our family was seated at an after-Christmas supper one year, a neighbor called with the news that Joshua and Jeremiah and Jessie were on the run. Kent was out of town for the holidays, so Daddy and my brother-in-law and I reluctantly pushed back from the mostly finished feast before us and charged out the door toward Daddy's old Chevrolet pickup, hoping to catch those wayward goats before they put too much distance between us.

We were too late.

A few miles down the road, a coon hunter standing on the edge of a thick growth of poplars said he had spotted them heading toward Calvary Baptist Church Road. With their biblical names I guess we should have anticipated that, especially with it being Christmas. But when we arrived at Calvary, they had moved on. It doesn't take much church for some folks, and I guess goats are no different.

Next, we stopped by the house of a man who raised goats of his own. "Yeah, they stopped by for a short visit but left in a hurry. Guess they had other goats to call on for the holidays," and he laughed as if he had said something funny.

Nothing was amusing to us since we had left Mother's table of delicious food not fully satisfied. I can't even bear mentioning the untouched desserts of meringue-covered chocolate pies, pineapple upside-down cake, and numerous other assorted goodies we had abandoned in order to ramble around the dark countryside chasing three independent-minded, buffet-craving goats.

We were about out of search options when I was startled to hear that plaintive cry from my father: "Jeremiah! Jeremiah! Jeremiah!" Risking a glimpse upward out of the corner of my right eye, I failed to catch a glimpse of the weeping prophet, but Daddy's desperate plea must have had effect since we suddenly spotted all three goats moving along the tree line of a weed-covered field they were leisurely mowing.

Cautiously, we eased up behind them, realizing that in our haste to leave we had failed to bring lead ropes. Someone asked us later why we didn't use our belts. Funny how in the moment of crisis we often overlook the simplest solutions.

So now we began herding those obstinate goats over four miles of dark, uneven terrain, illuminated only by the dim headlights of Daddy's old pickup and a moon that sporadically peeped from behind passing clouds. Neither light was sufficient.

My brother-in-law and I would jump off the narrow running boards on each side of the truck every couple minutes to steer those obstinate goats in approximately the right direction. During that frustrating journey home, I discovered that goats do not like to be herded or told what to do.

At one point I called out, "Joshua, you were chosen by God Almighty to take over for Moses and lead the people of Israel into the promised land. Lead us home, Joshua, lead us home!" (Josh 1:6).

Joshua had no interest in my Sunday school lesson, nor in his namesake, as he led us across deep side ditches from which we emerged with mouthfuls of dirt and weeds and skinned knees. Further ignoring my pleas, the goats took us down dark, dirt driveways alive with menacing growls and barks from protective farm dogs, such a circuitous route that at least four miles were added to our difficult trip home.

Finally, I had the definitive answer to a question a little eight-year-old girl had asked me during a pastor's class in which I was teaching the tenets of the Christian faith: "Why did Jesus call the bad people 'goats'?"

She was referring, of course, to Matthew's account of how those who did not follow Jesus' command to feed the hungry, clothe the naked, and visit the prisoners were asked to stand with the goats on his left. Now I knew. And it had nothing at all to do with the ancient folklore that associated goats with the devil, although at that moment I could certainly understand how that particular folk tale got started.

It was as simple as this: Goats insist on going their own way.

Jeremiah, Joshua, and Jessie refused every direction we suggested as they continually bobbed their heads, looking for an escape, a way out, intent on going their own way.

Evidently, Jesus had seen a lot of folks just like that, called it "goat-like," and made it clear that such behavior had no place in his kingdom (Matt 25:41–43).

We finally made it home that night. But as I dragged my exhausted body into bed, I renewed my determination to keep listening for a voice on the way to Mullinix, on the way to allowing God's kingdom to come fully in me. It was certain I could not reach my destination by going my own way.

As I turned out the lights and closed my eyes, I tried to express thanks for those goats for that reminder. But the words stuck in my throat.

It wasn't long after that my brother sold Jeremiah, Joshua, and Jessie. When their purpose for being became more trouble than it was worth, it was time for them to go.

While "going to Mullinix," I try hard to escape that same judgment.

Part Four

Family Life

From Playhouse to Horror House
to Playhouse

My wife and I walked into the Playhouse Theatre at Walt Disney World on the second day of our visit there with our daughter, Cheryl, her husband, Steve, and their four children, our grandchildren. Kayla, Austin, and Christian, the three oldest children, thought the Playhouse was too childish and were reluctant to enter. But we did it for Cameron. We owed him.

As hard as we tried not to do anything "scary" for a four-year-old, we failed miserably on several occasions. Our worst failure was when we walked into a show titled "Honey, I Shrunk the Kids," in which all kinds of unidentified critters played around our feet in absolute darkness and an unknown liquid sprinkled down on us. I looked over to see Cameron's eyes wide open, his mouth readied for a scream.

Instead of screaming, however, he placed his hands over his ears, shut his eyes tight, and ducked under the seats, where he remained until the end of the show when the lights came back on.

Walking out of the show hoping Cameron had not been so emotionally traumatized that it would cripple him for life, we ran into Steve and the other two boys who had stopped at the racetrack.

"How was the show?" they asked.

"Well," I started to reply before Cameron interrupted with enthusiasm, "It was great! I put my hands over my ears, shut my eyes real tight, and crawled under the seats and didn't see anything. It was great!"

Like I said, we owed Cameron. So we folded our creaking knees, at least mine were creaking, and sat on the floor trying to become children again for at least the 30 minutes of the Playhouse show.

Mr. Rogers would have been proud. Disney characters were leading us in popular children's songs as all the children were dancing to the music, just dancing all around us. I felt my inner child fighting hard to break through the hardened shell of my adulthood, and if not exactly jumping up and joining the swirl of dancing children, I wanted to at least struggle to my feet and sway in place, which according to my children is the only kind of dancing I've ever done.

Just then I noticed a young boy of maybe 12 sitting in a wheelchair, surrounded by three happy little girls younger than the boy, but whom I assumed were his sisters. The wheelchair-bound boy tried to join them in clapping to the music, but his hands would not cooperate, flailing in all directions but never quite touching to complete the clap his mind had envisioned.

Watching more closely but trying not to stare, I saw that his eyes were also having trouble focusing on the Disney characters dancing in front of his wheelchair. His eyes jerked from side to side, unable to pause on any one spot, and his mouth tried again and again to sing the songs with his sisters, but his crooked lips refused to form the shapes that would yield intelligible words.

That was the most frightening thing I had seen all day. Such harsh reality crashing the party of this fantasy world. So much pain in the middle of all that joy. For an instant I wanted, like Cameron, to shut my eyes real tight, put my hands over my ears, and duck out of sight.

I've known many such places on the way to Mullinix. But "closing my eyes and hiding" are neither viable options nor a healthy way to live as we grow older. Confronting and overcoming are the expectations for grownups.

Suddenly, escape became unnecessary as the boy's father, sitting beside the wheelchair, unwound his long, skinny legs and, standing behind his son, took the restless hands into his steady hands. Together they did an arm dance in rhythm to the music. I felt my eyes grow moist as the father guided his son's hands toward each other, meeting in a loud clap and then another and another and another. I didn't want it to end. Why does clapping always end too soon? A crooked smile crept onto the boy's lips, not like the pretty smiles of his sisters, but I could tell it was most definitely a smile, and I was certain his joy was no less than that of all the other dancing children.

I closed my eyes and uttered a silent prayer of thanksgiving that living on this side of the cross, I don't have to shut my eyes and cover my ears and run away from the scary things that wait to ambush me around every corner.

At the very least the resurrection means I can confront fear and pain and bodies that won't work right, trusting that God will take my trembling hands into his steady hands and bring them together in a delighted clap, especially when I am too tired and hopeless to clap for myself.

So I'm able to continue my journey toward a higher plane of discipleship, comforted by the words of our risen Lord: "Do not be afraid. Go and tell my brothers to go to Galilee; there they will see me" (Matt 28:10).

I like to think that also means I will be able to see him more clearly when I reach Mullinix even though I've had "signs" of his presence all along the way— signs that have soothed my fears enough that I am able to face them with my eyes wide open as I take the next step.

Waiting for the Boil

The stranger's shoulders drooped in disappointment as he said, "I've been coming here for six years and still haven't seen a boil." I was determined that it wouldn't happen to us.

When we arrived at Holden Beach, North Carolina, for a week of vacation with our children and grandchildren, the little island was boiling with excitement and anticipation. Two months before our arrival, those enormous endangered loggerhead sea turtles had lumbered across the beach, leaving bulldozer-like tracks in the white sand to lay the first eggs of the nesting season.

Now it was time to make preparations for the first boil. We are not always able to control the right time or even predict the right time when it suddenly comes. All we can do is be prepared at all times.

Besides, big things often come as a surprise. We had planned our vacation with no knowledge of the unusual, exciting events about to take place, and yet we were right on time for one of our most enjoyable vacation weeks ever.

A charming, hospitable couple, Sydney and Travis Meadow, who had adopted the nest at the end of our pier, told us it was called a "boil" because when those tiny turtles break through the egg shells and start a mad fight to the top, they resemble a frenetically boiling pot of water.

Now, finally, it was the right time, and careful preparations were being made. First of all, we had been instructed to dig a shallow trench from the nest to the surf. The grandchildren used their plastic shovels, and we grownups were using a couple regular-sized shovels provided by the Meadows. Red cloth squares were cut and distributed to all the families to cover our flashlights as we aided the tiny turtles in making their way to their home in the sea.

In a perfect world our little lights would not be necessary since their creator had equipped those tiny newborn turtles with irresistible instincts to send them scurrying toward the light of the moon reflecting off the shifting surf about 75 yards from the nest.

But now we had to help them find their way, attempting to correct our careless interference with nature through the installation of so many artificial lights along the beach that the little turtles became confused in their search for the true light that pointed them toward home.

Seems like we still do that year after year, constructing new lights that promise life but only leave us more confused.

But it was time, and preparations had to be made. Not satisfied with the protection afforded by the chicken wire that had been placed over the nest to protect the eggs from predators, diligent human guards brought out chairs and blankets to watch the nests throughout the long night. No exact time could be predicted, but most boils occur between 8:00 p.m. and 4:00 a.m.

Two houses down, the excitement was at a peak since the eggs in their nest had been laid two days before ours. That Wednesday night, 200 people gathered around the nest in readiness.

Somewhere around 11:45, however, after an afternoon of playing on the beach in 95-degree heat, all but a handful of hardy souls retired to their air-conditioned bedrooms. Just after midnight, 119 turtles were born in that neighboring nest and made their eager, twisting crawl to their new home and their only chance to perpetuate the species.

Those who had given up too soon and missed the seminal moment were as frustrated and disappointed as the man who told me he had been coming to this beach for six years and had never seen a boil.

"Did you wait by the nest all night?" I asked. "No," he admitted reluctantly. "I was always too drained by the sun and, after drinking a couple beers, went to bed early." Year after year, he was disappointed and frustrated and angry because he lacked the endurance to wait long enough.

Luke's Gospel reads, "You also must be ready, for the Son of Man is coming at an unexpected hour" (12:40). There is a clear warning in this apocalyptic passage—a warning for those of us not ready for our Lord's appearance.

But most of us hear only what we want to hear. Like most three-year-olds, our grandson, Christian, had very selective hearing during that vacation week. "Come here right now!" his mother called impatiently. "That's the third time I've called you!" With an angelic smile Christian looked up at his mother and said, "No, Mama, that's the fourth time you called me."

On Thursday evening, a ghost crab invaded our nest. The Meadows told us someone was going in that night to get the crab and that the attempted extraction would probably start the boil.

I wasn't pleased to hear that news since it sounded like induced labor to me, and I was told by a young doctor in Raleigh, North Carolina, after Jean and I had waited three-and-a-half weeks beyond the due date for the birth of our first child, that waiting for nature to take its course is usually best.

We waited and were rewarded with a beautiful baby girl. So I'm a lifelong advocate of trusting the natural course of things, often avoiding doctors or delaying visiting them because "often the body will heal itself if we are patient."

But I was not invited to share an opinion on the turtle births, so we watched as the turtle midwife carefully inserted her hand into the nest to retrieve the ghost crab. Sure enough, it happened just as Sydney Meadow had predicted.

"I can't find the crab," the woman said, withdrawing her hand, "but here comes the first turtle!"

With much anticipation we craned our necks to see those first tiny turtles boil to the surface. When our children were born, it was not common medical practice for the father to be allowed into the birthing room, so this was new for me.

Sydney Meadow picked the baby turtles up one by one, examined them, and placed them in the trench, where our grandchildren, along with Stella, a pretty blonde little girl from next door, stood in readiness with their red cloth-covered flashlights to guide the little turtles toward a chance at life.

What a reward for all the waiting and preparing! It was a deeply spiritual experience as we played a small part in the mystery and magnificence of God's ongoing creation.

So this passage from Luke is not only a warning to the unprepared but a great promise for those ready for his unexpected appearance, offering an unparalleled gift: "Fear not, little flock, for it is your Father's good pleasure to give you the kingdom" (Luke 12:32).

We were prepared. When the word had gone out that the nest was in full boil, we had our flashlights ready and our party clothes on and even refreshments for the children who were staying up long past their bedtime.

We were prepared, and when word came, the excited voice of little three-year-old Christian sent us all rushing toward the beach. "Come on peoples!" he cried. "Nana's got the juice. Let's go see the toitles!"

At every point along the way to Mullinix, I need to be ready for a party. The boil could begin at any time.

A Small Man?

The first rays of morning light were bursting through the night darkness as the District of Columbia police officer approached a suspicious-looking small man dozing with his head resting on the back of the driver's seat in the blue 1957 Buick. The early morning light was slowly spreading across the almost deserted downtown sidewalks, awaiting the rush of pedestrians hurrying to work.

Knocking on the side window and motioning for the sleepy driver to lower the side window, the officer said, "Sir, could I see your license?"

As the man drowsily fumbled for his wallet in a back pants pocket, the policeman continued, "What are you doing parked here so early in the morning?"

Handing the officer his license, the man replied with a mischievous smile, "Waiting for a pig."

Believing he might soon be taking the man to the nearest mental hospital, the officer hesitantly returned the license and walked slowly back to his squad car, where he watched and waited.

Within 30 minutes a farm truck from Loudoun County, Virginia, pulled up behind the blue Buick. The short man got out, and he and the farmer lifted a slippery pink pig, fully dressed, out of the back of the pickup and deposited him on the back seat of the car. Pedestrians who were now rapidly filling the sidewalks crashed into each other as they turned to take a startled second look at a pig in a Buick smiling at them grotesquely through the back window.

The small man handed a few bills to the farmer, waved pleasantly to the open-mouthed police officer, and headed back toward his restaurant in Bethesda, Maryland, to begin the task of transforming the pig into vinegar and pepper-based eastern North Carolina barbecue for his expectant clientele.

Sometimes it was difficult to determine what Angelo Alton ("Shorty") Edwards enjoyed more: feeding people or making them laugh. Customers also had trouble deciding whether they came to the restaurant mostly to see Shorty or eat his high-quality food straight off the farm. Shorty insisted on using only the best meat, buying freshly cut chuck roasts and grinding them to make his famous hamburgers.

Going to Mullinix

Shorty was born in eastern North Carolina and graduated from the University of North Carolina as an undefeated wrestler and aspiring pharmacist. But like a lot of folks during WWII, he moved to the Washington, DC, area, where the action seemed to be concentrated during that period of our nation's history.

It did not take long, however, for Shorty to discover that he had more passion for people than pushing pills at People's drugstore. Shorty's other passion was food, so he chose to combine these passions by opening restaurants in the downtown area of the District of Columbia.

In the beginning his restaurants were named Transit Hamburger Shops 1 and 2. Soon, Shorty sold those and opened a restaurant on Georgia Avenue, where he started his family with his wife, Mary Robert, in a one-bedroom apartment over the hamburger shop.

A customer came running into the shop at the busy lunch hour one day and asked excitedly, "Shorty, how many children do you have?"

"Four so far," Shorty replied proudly."

"Well," the man said, "I think one of them is lying on the sidewalk outside."

It was the type of prank Shorty often pulled on his customers, and he wondered briefly if they were turning the tables on him. But taking no chances, he raced outside and found his youngest, Frances, lying in front of the shop seemingly unharmed after falling two stories to the concrete sidewalk.

With children tumbling out of windows, Shorty decided he needed a bigger place for his growing family, so he moved them to Silver Spring, Maryland, and opened another hamburger shop in Bethesda, naturally called "Shorty's," where he remained until his retirement 30 years later.

One day I watched a well-dressed young executive tumble backward off a bar stool in an attempt to avoid the ketchup "accidentally" squirted toward his white shirt. Of course, it was only a red string flying out of the red plastic container Shorty had carefully contrived.

Day-old hard rolls thrown from the front door toward friends passing by served as greeting cards. Once, he threw a roll into a passing police car with its windows open. Instead of stopping, they continued on about their business knowing Shorty had just said "hello."

Free hamburgers were for anyone who guessed what was changing around the shop. One change no one ever guessed was that the 5'1" Shorty was growing taller every day. Each late afternoon after the shop closed, Shorty would walk to the shoe repair store down the street and have one-half inch added to the soles of his shoes.

Probably no one ever guessed that one because Shorty was always larger in their eyes than his physical stature.

During summer 1964 when I married his oldest daughter, Jean, I saw a man sitting at a table against the far wall drop a glass that Shorty had thrown at him across the bar. Fragments of the shattered glass lay scattered on the green table top and seat. Perhaps it was the man's first visit to "Shorty's" and he wasn't aware of the daily mantra: "If you want some water, sucker, catch this."

After sneaking out from behind the counter where he had ducked, Shorty turned to me red-faced and said, "That's the first one that's been dropped in 30 years."

Maybe, finally, Shorty had not thrown it just right, because not long afterward, Shorty sold the shop and retired. When the reflexes of an undefeated amateur wrestler and an unequaled professional jokester start to go, maybe it's time to hang it up.

But a person with Shorty's irresistible spirit finds it difficult to retire from pulling his tricks. Our children remember shopping with their grandfather and hiding behind a wall as they watched people scramble for the coins Shorty had secretly thrown at their feet. Their laughter only increased as the startled crowd frantically checked their pockets for holes.

Shorty also had a nickel, which thrilled our children. In the beginning he asked them to lean closely and see if they could tell him the date. "My eyes aren't what they used to be." When their faces were up against the nickel, their grandfather pressed the back of the coin and filled their straining eyes with a quick squirt of water. After squealing with laughter, they begged him to try it on others, even complete strangers.

Of course, Shorty obliged. A born jokester never fully retires.

Thoreau used to sit by Walden Pond and think about how most people lead lives of quiet desperation, eating, sleeping, working, and growing old—not really noticing what is going on around them and missing most of the important things.

Much earlier, Jesus had said that most of the people he met "though seeing, they do not see; though hearing they do not hear or understand" (Matt 13:13). Jesus' words appear to be directed primarily at our inability to perceive and understand the "secrets" of the kingdom that had come to earth in him.

I think he may have also been referring to our lack of seeing and appreciating the many hidden treasures of life—such as the laughter and joy around us all the time—which often require unique individuals like Shorty Edwards to penetrate our blindness and deafness.

Shorty had a sign in front of his shop that read, "If you can't come in, smile when you go by."

"Jerry," he told me one day, "I want that sign in front of my coffin."

When I officiated at his funeral in 1998, we didn't have the sign, but our memories of Shorty made us smile and laugh as we passed by—not yet quite ready to come in but eternally grateful for the laughter he brought into our lives.

As I make my way toward Mullinix, people who open my eyes and ears to the laughter and joy of life help me experience the "first fruits" of the abundance awaiting at the end of the journey (Rom 8:23).

Someone who can help me accomplish that cannot be called a small man.

A Bloody Thanksgiving

With unusual agility, my eight-year-old granddaughter, Kayla, leaped up from her place on the rocking chair next to mine and charged through the front door, calling out in a panicked voice, "Mama, hurry! Papa's playing with his knife again!"

Earlier that morning, eager to show my grandchildren how proficient their Papa was with his brand-new Swiss Army knife, a recent gift from friends, I began confidently trimming small hickory limbs to use for roasting marshmallows around a bonfire that evening. It only took three swipes of the razor-sharp blade to open a deep, two-inch gash on top of my left-hand thumb.

So instead of being amazed at my skill, my grandchildren were horrified by the blood flowing down my palm onto the ground, turning the multicolored fall leaves an ugly deep brown. My intrigued audience had run screaming for help. It wasn't the reaction I'd been aiming for.

My wife and I had traveled to Brandon, Mississippi, 10 miles outside of Jackson, to spend Thanksgiving with our daughter and her family. Cheryl's husband, Steve, thought it would be fun for the family to spend one night and two days at a campground owned by the Presbyterian churches of Jackson, where he had taken his church youth group on a retreat a few months earlier.

The camp turned out to be a gorgeous 423-acre chunk of some of God's best work. The weather was perfect with the welcome taste of a cool Mississippi fall in the air.

Determined to take advantage of every available opportunity, we propelled across the twin lakes on canoes, fished out of john boats, and sat cross-legged on small rafts as our grandchildren ferried us across the water to a small island in the middle of the largest lake.

Swings hanging from tall oak trees gave us a sense of being one with the sky and flying with the eagles. Rope bridges dangling over deep gullies tested our sense of adventure, and when we wanted to simply sit and reflect, we had our pick of two dozen white rocking chairs populating the porch, which encircled three-fourths of the large white clapboard house.

It was a perfect place to spend Thanksgiving, and our son-in-law spoke for all of us when he said, "This is the way life is supposed to be." We were content and thankful.

But toward late afternoon on our first full day, we decided to have a cookout with hamburgers and hot dogs, followed by a marshmallow roast. "I think there are some clothes hangers in our bedroom closets for the hot dogs and marshmallows," Cheryl said helpfully.

"Oh no," I protested emphatically, certain I was being even more helpful. "We need sweet-smelling, freshly trimmed hickory boughs for an authentic marshmallow roast."

So began the misadventure of the sliced thumb. Responding to the frightened cries of the grandchildren, clearly traumatized by the stream flowing from my sliced thumb, the rest of the family rushed over offering their solution to my wound, most agreeing that I should have the deep cut closed with stitches.

"Did Daniel Boone or Davy Crockett run to First Med at the first sight of blood?" I asked indignantly, ignoring Kayla's whispered question to her oldest brother, seven-year-old Austin, "Who's Daniel Boone?" Continuing with my pioneer bravado I said, "Just find me a dirty rag to wrap it in, and let's get on with the twig trimming."

I must not have been very convincing because the next thing I knew, Steve had called the camp host, who arrived with a commercial-size first aid kit in hand. After examining my thumb despite my futile protests, he said, "There's a place up the road that we use to stitch up our young campers." I noticed that he was looking at the gray in my beard as he emphasized the word "young" with a crooked smile that was at least the first cousin to a smirk.

It didn't help my injured feelings when Steve spoke up in an apparent attempt to bolster my argument against stitches. "Well, I guess when you get to be Papa's age you don't worry about scars."

Nodding, our smiling young host turned toward the door and left with his first aid kit as I murmured, "Young smart alecks," while increasing the pressure on my thumb to slow the bleeding.

Later, when marshmallow-roasting time came, I remembered the twigs I had dropped at the edge of the forest. Carrying them to the porch, I again took out my Swiss Army knife to finish the trimming. That was when Kayla, possessing the strong maternal instincts that afflict many first-born siblings, had seen enough and raised the alarm: "Papa's playing with his knife again!"

Family came rushing out of every door with handfuls of coat hangers already straightened to hold the hot dogs and marshmallows over the fire. As the sun began to set behind the tall trees and the campfire dwindled to marshmallow-roasting size, I was a little hurt that I was the only one holding a slightly discolored hickory stick.

Well, I tried, even if my efforts did end up in a bloody mess. I gave it my best shot, and sometimes that's the best we can do and all that's expected of us.

Reflecting on his success in building the temple and providing a home for the ark of the covenant, a feat his father was unable to accomplish, King Solomon said, "My father David had it in his heart to build a temple for the Name of the LORD, the God of Israel. But the LORD said to my father David, 'Because it was in your heart to build a temple for my Name, you did well to have this in your heart'" (1 Kgs 8:17–18).

On the road to Mullinix, attempting to build a temple of authentic discipleship, I understand the task can become difficult and sometimes I am left bruised and bloodied. But if I sincerely desire kingdom living—if, like David, I "have it in my heart"—I trust that God is pleased with my efforts even if I don't make it all the way.

I Want You Where I Can See You

While visiting our daughter and her family in North Augusta, South Carolina, I took my two oldest grandsons, Austin and Christian, and one of their friends to see the Augusta Greenjackets, a low A farm club of the Boston Red Sox.

We had a great time getting autographs (no sports figure ranks too low when it comes to young boys getting autographs), eating expensive hot dogs (no hot dog is too expensive as long as it has chili, mustard, coleslaw and minced onions), pink mounds of cotton candy, heavily salted peanuts, and 16-ounce soft drinks. Well, we weren't there for our health.

Being a sports fan in the fullest meaning of that word—as in "fanatic"—I was enjoying watching the action on the field while the boys were hanging over the fence down the first base line hoping to catch a foul ball or persuading the bullpen players to toss them a scuffed ball.

But along about the seventh-inning stretch, Christian and his friend had found some of their buddies, and they were becoming restless. Together, they ran up to where I was sitting on the twelfth row of the grandstand. Christian was the assigned spokesman for the group. "Papa," he said, "we want to go behind the stands and pitch."

That presented me with a dilemma. Austin was still hanging on to the fence watching the game, so if I went with Christian and his friends, I would no longer be able to keep my eye on Austin. This might not seem like much of a problem to some folks, but for an overprotective grandfather it was a real dilemma.

Even though it was a low A farm club playing an inconsequential game, it was North Augusta recreation night, so all the little leaguers and their parents and coaches were there, a large crowd of people in which it would be easy to lose three young boys. I'm real funny about wanting to go home with the same number of boys I bring to sports events.

I reluctantly told Christian, "Son, I'm sorry, but I'd rather you stayed on this side of the stands. I want you where I can see you."

That seemed to satisfy Christian as he quickly said, "Okay," and ran back to once again hang over the fence with his friends, all within my line of sight.

I always seem to remember this little incident every time Ascension Day comes around. The book of Acts records the day when two men in white came to stand beside the disciples as they "looked intently" into the sky. "Men of Galilee," they said, "why do you stand here looking into the sky?" (Acts 1:10–11).

They were looking because Luke says Jesus had ascended into the clouds. Who wouldn't be looking and wondering why he was leaving them again after having just returned to walk with them once more following the resurrection?

But that's a very reassuring scene for me. I like to think of the ascension as if Jesus is saying, "I want you where I can see you." No longer restricted by time and space, his eyes are always on us. He has positioned himself so that I will never be lost in a crowd.

That chases the loneliness that often creeps in on the journey to Mullinix when the Christ I'm seeking to know fully seems to have temporarily gone away.

A Persistent Light

Funny how the greatest joys hold the potential for terrible tragedy.

Christmas morning is always warm and exciting when children are young and their faces are flush with anticipation. When my daughter's four children were small, and our only grandchildren at the time, Cheryl and her husband, Steve, would journey to Williamsburg with their young brood to spend Christmas with their Haywood grandparents.

One of our traditions was for Papa to get up before anyone else, put the sausage and egg casserole in the oven, turn on the coffee pot, start the fire in the fireplace, and yell up the steps, "You won't believe what happened last night! Santa Claus left a bunch of gifts under the tree!" Then I would step out of the way as a stampede of four pairs of small feet ensued.

On this particular morning, the routine was interrupted by near tragedy.

One of our close friends in the church who had been one of the few present when I arrived as a green young pastor on May 1, 1969, Lorene Hooker, a fellow Tar Heel who understood such things, had given me some rich pine-knot kindling with the warning not to use too much at one time.

But it was Christmas, and I was eager to have a large, warm fire to set the stage for another fantastic family Christmas morning. Besides, it was cold, and I wanted a quick, hot fire, so I placed one medium-sized and then one small piece of kindling underneath the dry hickory logs. That was one-and-a-half pieces too many.

A sudden fire exploded in a roar and began racing in billowing sheets up the chimney, where it ignited the creosote and other flammable materials coating the inside of the chimney. Running outside, I was terrified to see flames reaching toward the sky from the top of the chimney depositing little flaming splinters on the roof.

The folly of procrastination filled me with regret as I watched the small fireballs land on the leaves I had failed to blow off the roof despite my wife's constant reminders. Instinctively, I prayed perhaps the most common prayer that escapes the lips of frail humanity: "Help!"

Fighting the urge to call firemen out on a cold Christmas morning, I hurried back inside to fill a pitcher of water and pour it on the fire. I could not control the fire in the chimney, but at least I could put out the flames I could reach. Much of life is like that—so much we can't control and must simply wait for it to burn itself out—but we can act on that part within our reach.

"Can we come down now?" an eager child's voice called from the top of the stairs. "Not yet," I yelled over my right shoulder. "I have to put out the fire!"

Soon, the flames in the fireplace were extinguished, dripping water onto the growing flood at the bottom, but I heard the fire I could not reach still roaring up the chimney.

Another tiny voice, which I identified as Austin, the oldest grandson, called out, "Is Santa Claus all right?"

"Santa Claus is fine," I yelled back. "He left before the fire started." I could hear the sighs of relief all the way down the stairs.

Then I uttered my own sigh of relief as I realized the roar up the chimney was diminishing and finally felt free to call everyone downstairs for the opening of gifts. Waiting for the shuffling commotion upstairs to reach the den, I looked with both relief and regret at the sad spectacle of a wet, cold fireplace. We wouldn't have our warm fire this Christmas, but the warmth of a safe family would be more than enough.

Suddenly, I noticed a small splinter of wood, still lit, floating on the pool of water collecting on the floor of the fireplace from the dripping hickory logs.

That persistent little floating flame remains a symbol of Christmas for me.

As a young pastor I would become frustrated and dejected that I was called out to so many sad and tragic events in the lives of our church family at Christmas. "Why Christmas? Why do such things have to happen at Christmas?" But as the years passed, my question changed to "Why not Christmas?"

Why not Christmas when the light no darkness can put out shines the brightest? Jesus said, "I am the light of the world. Whoever follows me will never walk in darkness, but will have the light of life" (John 8:12).

So many fearful things threaten to steal our joy and peace and celebration each Christmas, but the light of Christ remains a hope that no darkness on this earth can extinguish.

Following that light remains my only chance of reaching Mullinix.

River Journeying

Rivers have always held a special attraction for me, so the 100-acre plot my mother inherited from her father, which he had inherited from his ancestors, became my special healing place during the busy years as pastor of a growing church. Some of my best healing times have taken place beside and on rivers, fishing, hiking, watching, and simply waiting on God.

Symbolically, rivers have stood for movement. Rivers call us to a journey, sometimes an irresistible journey, as the rushing water cuts through earth and rock, refusing to be halted. Sometimes the journey is inward as we seek the hidden place where we meet God and are moved forward on our journey of faith.

A river journey that brings warm memories was one I took with my father many years ago. We had been fishing from the pier beside the little cabin he had built on a little peninsula in the vortex of Little River and a little creek when I asked if we could see how far up the river we could go.

I was aware that in one direction, not far away, was the dam my father crossed on foot many times in the dark of night when he was courting my mother. ("Courting" still sounds more romantic to me than "hanging.")

The dam-crossing shortened Daddy's trip by many miles since Mother lived on one side of the river and Daddy on the other. But the flat cement crown of the dam, which alternately trapped and freed the river water, providing electricity for the community, looked precariously narrow.

"Daddy," I said one day when we ventured near the dam in a little john boat. "That's a mighty narrow ledge to cross in the dark."

He chuckled softly. "Most of the time my flashlight worked. Other times I felt my way along."

"You must have thought Mother was worth the risk," I teased. Daddy chuckled again and said, "Yeah, guess I did."

His generation was not given to gushing. My father's most exuberant compliment was, "It's fine." Sometimes, my mother tried hard to get more out of him, such as, "That is really good! The best I've ever eaten!" No matter how hard she tried, Daddy's response was always, "It's fine." For him, "fine" was the pinnacle of compliments.

We were quiet as we floated near the dam on the little electric motor-propelled john boat, and I knew he was fondly recalling those early years before they began a long, loving marriage that only ended with my father's death 62 years later.

Daddy was also familiar with the river in the direction leading away from the dam since he and his family of origin lived on a steep hill extending up from the river a short distance downriver. Daddy would often tell of catching fish with his hands by reaching up under the overhanging banks or seining for fish with a burlap sheet attached to a pole on each end when a church fish supper at Calvary Baptist Church was scheduled.

On this day, my father seemed as excited about my request for the river exploration adventure as I was, quickly falling into the role of tour guide, pointing out the names of the various creeks and reciting the names of the landowners along both sides of the river.

His eyes lost their customary twinkle when he pointed out one thickly wooded tract of land on our left that two brothers had fought over.

"Couldn't agree on the boundary line no matter how many times it got surveyed," Daddy said quietly. "People had to be mighty tight with their money back then, but they always seemed to find enough for surveys." He chuckled ironically before continuing, "Heard one of them say he couldn't wait to dump the first shovelful of dirt into his brother's face as he lay in his grave." The other brother, in a rare moment of self-reflection, told my father, "I dus tell ya, Johnie. That lil' piece o' land's gonna send me and John both to hell."

Dipping his oar a little deeper into the muddy water to give the electric motor a little assistance, Daddy shook his head slowly at the painful memories. "Didn't speak to each other for 15 years. One passed away during the silent years, but I never did hear if his brother grabbed the first shovel at the cemetery."

Again, he was silent for a moment before adding, "Now they're both gone, and nobody cares about the boundary line anymore. All that time wasted over a passing thing like a few feet of land. Guess they thought a little more land would give them some sort of permanence."

Daddy paused again. He never did make long speeches, and this one had already gone on longer than usual. "But as far as I could tell, it didn't add one minute of life to either brother."

We paddled along in silence for a while with only the quiet background drone of the small electric motor, each of us lost in our private thoughts of the transitory nature of life and how our worry over insignificant things consumes us and destroys our lives and our families.

In spots, the river would become so shallow and rocky that we would have to take off our shoes and roll up the legs of our jeans and lift the john boat over the protruding hills of rock and silt until we could drop it into deeper water on the other side.

Coming around one bend in the river, we startled a small brown wood duck who flew into panic mode at our unexpected appearance before gathering himself and disappearing into the thick woods. Up ahead, just beyond the bend, we wandered into an idyllic creek with low-hanging limbs, which we gently brushed out of the way.

"Beavers been busy in here," Daddy said suddenly, and I looked down to see a small pole completely stripped of bark floating on the surface of the water.

I reached down to pull it into the boat. "As much material as those beavers have to work with out here, they won't miss this," I said, eager to take it home and show my children and tell them about my river journey with their grandfather. The total time of the trip was probably no more than four or five hours, but my warm memories have lasted a lifetime.

My father died on Valentine's Day in 1999, but every time I visit a river or climb into a boat of any kind and size, I hear his voice, subdued and reverent, as if he were in an outdoor cathedral, identifying points of interest along the way and sharing his knowledge of the ways of life in the places he had traveled many years before my birth.

Those memories and that voice still bring me much comfort and encouragement when the way grows difficult. I guess that's something of what the author of Hebrews meant when he wrote, "Therefore, since we are surrounded by such a great cloud of witnesses, let us throw off everything that hinders and the sin that so easily entangles, and let us run with perseverance the race marked out for us" (Heb 12:1).

I need all those voices of strong people from the past pointing the way they have traveled before me and shouting words of encouragement when my steps start to falter.

If "going to Mullinix," that place of authentic kingdom living, was a solitary journey, I don't think I would make it.

Too Old to Eat Cornbread

The thing you need to understand about North Carolina mothers is that they understand neither the dangers of obesity nor the value of a diet. Feeding is an act of love, and to refuse food is a rejection of love.

So I tried to plan my visits to my parents' home in Mt. Gilead at those times when I was not on one of my periodic diets. Besides, I hated them as much as Mother did. Diets always leave me slightly depressed, and I wanted to be at my best in order to give Mother a lift when I made my too infrequent visits home.

On one particular trip soon after my father's death, my goal was to get Mother out of the house. True to form, Mother had made several dozen yeast rolls before my arrival, and we decided to distribute them to various family members.

Those were the same rolls Daddy took every day to his younger brother, Branson, when he had been confined to bed during his final bleak months with cancer. Mother's yeast rolls were the only food Branson would eat during that time, a few years before my father's battle with his own cancer.

"That's the only thing I can taste now," Branson told Daddy. At least being able to taste homemade rolls was a great blessing since he had always enjoyed good food as much as I do. It's a genetic thing, I guess.

Boiled okra, however, did not fall within Branson's list of good food. One day around noon, I was sitting at the little bar between the kitchen and the dining room at my parents' home when Uncle Branson walked in with his eyes alert to whatever Mother was cooking that day. Most of our kin always seemed to time their visits when they knew Mother would be cooking—which was most of the time.

On this day, she was cooking boiled okra, one of the few things she prepared just for herself. Mother had finally given up on chittlins when I reached 12 years of age and told her I could no longer enjoy them with her. The pungent smell of those scrubbed white intestines frying finally became more than I could tolerate. So now boiled okra was the only dish she continued to cook for herself.

The rest of the family preferred Mother's crisp fried okra chopped into small pieces and rolled generously in corn meal before being dumped into a pan filled

Going to Mullinix

with hot, melted Crisco or, in earlier days, homemade lard. Like us, Branson found boiled okra too slick and slimy for his taste.

Mother knew this, but she said teasingly as she slurped down another long pod of softly steamed okra, "Branson, pull up a chair and help me eat this boiled okra." Watching her with a wrinkled nose and emphatic shake of his head, Branson said, "Thank you just the same, Ina. But I make it a policy to avoid food I have to cross my legs to eat."

Oh, but he loved those yeast rolls Daddy brought faithfully until the day he died. I was saddened that Branson was not around to return the favor when Daddy lay in his own bed dying of prostate cancer.

On this day, Mother and I gathered up those famous yeast rolls and took a few to her older sister, Lannie, who had checked herself into a nursing home in Mt. Gilead. That was one of the few times I have experienced anyone moving voluntarily into a nursing home so that her children would not have to make that difficult decision. I admired her for it.

Lannie's hair was still wet from a recent shower when we walked into her room. "I'm as mad as a wet settin' hen," she said loudly before we even said "hello." "I didn't want a shower, but they won't let you decide nothin' f' yourself 'round here."

Sitting on the edge of her sister's bed, Mother took the cloth off the rolls, and for a few minutes that rich, yeasty aroma disguised the urine-saturated smell of the nursing home. Lannie's eyes brightened, and a smile quickly replaced her scowl. "Brought you something," Mother said, holding out the rolls.

The transforming power of Mother's food was clearly demonstrated right before our eyes as Lannie bit into the first roll, consuming most of it with one bite. It was a wonder to behold the change in her attitude, which completely transformed the atmosphere of the room. I had seen Mother's food exert that power many times through the years, but it always brought a sense of amazement and deep gratitude.

That's probably the main reason I have such a distaste for diets. Eating together is much more than ingesting food. For my family of origin, at least, it was a primary cultural rite of intimate bonding and sharing and loving.

After spending an hour with Lannie, we drove over to Chip, the little community about eight miles out in the country, where Mother and her family grew up. Mother's brother G. A. still lived in the home place across from the country store, which had been the commercial and social hub of the community since the mid-20s.

One reason I wanted to visit was to pick up a zucchini squash apple pie recipe from G. A.'s wife, Helen, a recipe I had heard folks raving about.

Thoughtful church members had been leaving so much zucchini in the back seat of our car after church every Sunday morning that we had run out of uses for it and had begun locking our car doors. After hearing about this recipe, however, I called my wife, Jean, and told her to leave the doors unlocked this Sunday because I was coming home with a new zucchini recipe.

While we were visiting G. A. and Helen, another of Mother's four sisters, Stella, called and asked us to stay over for supper. Stella and her husband, Lester, had moved from their house at the end of the road, which ran uphill beside "Haywood's Grocery," to a smaller home on the banks of Little River.

Seems they had caught some fish off their pier earlier that morning and wanted us to come help eat them. I could help with that.

"Mother," I said, "I know you're tired from your food delivery stops, but I sure would love some of those fresh fried fish and hushpuppies." I already had a suspicion that since food was involved, Mother would agree. So we drove up and then down the hilly gravel road leading to the banks of Little River.

The dining area in Lester and Stella's home actually dangled out over the river with the pier attached on the left. A gentle rain had started tapping against the large picture window, which offered a pleasant view of the river. As we sat down to a meal of fried fish—carefully filleted so we could eat faster and not have to worry so much about the bones—coleslaw with lots of mayonnaise and vinegar and salt and pepper, deep-fried hushpuppies, and a large slice of sweet Vidalia onion, I knew I had come home again.

Out of the corner of my eyes, I spotted a peach cobbler sitting on the counter behind Stella, in all its golden-brown splendor with little crystal droplets of sweet peach filling spilling out between the bottom and top layers of the homemade pie crusts. I could just feel the love oozing into my arteries.

We ate and talked and laughed leisurely for the next 45 minutes or so. All of Mother's family loved to tell stories and laugh, and Stella carried on that wonderful tradition with a deep-down belly laugh that was contagious.

I was thinking how perfect everything was when suddenly Lester began coughing and choking as his face turned a deep red. Stella jumped up to pound him on the back as Mother and I watched anxiously. I had been thinking I was going

Going to Mullinix

to have to apply my training in the Heimlich maneuver when Lester suddenly returned to normal breathing.

Tears streamed down his cheeks from the strain of it all when Lester looked over at me and smiled ironically as he gasped out, "Jerry, I 'member when folks used to ask how old a child was and the family would say, 'Oh, he's just about old enough to eat cornbread without choking.'" He paused to take a deep breath before continuing, "Guess I'm gettin' too old t' eat cornbread without choking."

Glancing over at the rain still bouncing off the large window, he concluded so softly we could barely hear, "Don't know where the time went." I was beginning to lose some folks, like Daddy and Branson, and others whom I dearly loved, and his words struck a nerve in my heart.

A scene we had looked at in a recent worship service flashed into my mind. Mary was expressing her great love for Jesus not by lavishing him with food, although since Jesus was once called a glutton, I assume he enjoyed good food. That was another thing I appreciated about him.

Mary, however, did not bake Jesus a peach cobbler. She showed her love by dousing Jesus' body with expensive perfume.

The disciples thought it all a big waste, what with so many poor folks around. But I really don't think that was their biggest concern, since even the best of us disciples seem to have many vested interests. So Jesus said, "The poor you will always have with you, and you can help them any time you want. But you will not always have me" (Mark 14:7).

A sense of urgency suddenly crashed the party of good food and a warm family gathering. I wanted to stop time and freeze this special moment. When we dug in to the peach cobbler a little later, it tasted delicious with its cinnamon-sprinkled brown crust. But I could not ignore the hint of mortality that irresistibly flavored each bite.

A few minutes later, as we began our return trip down the dusty road, I thought of how my journey to Mullinix must be lived to the fullest, each moment and each experience held as precious.

The time left for me to attain mature kingdom citizenship would end far too soon.

A Father's Love
and Healing Scars

"Daddy, can I ride on your back?" The cry came from my excited eight-year-old son, who was already sprinting down the pier toward me.

"Sure!" I called out, bending my knees so my back was low enough for him to reach with an exuberant leap. But just as I reached a crouching position, I cried out, "No!" It was too late. Chris was already in midflight, heading directly toward the open knife in my back pocket.

Our children—Cheryl, 10; Chris, 8; and Brian, 3—had been having a great time, along with Jean and me, crabbing and fishing at a campground on a creek somewhere along the Chesapeake Bay. Church friends of ours had left their camper in place following their week's stay so we could have this family time.

The weather had been perfect and the fishing and crabbing good. Crabbing seemed to be our children's favorite activity, as they could hardly contain their excitement while slowly pulling in the crabs hungrily feasting on the chicken parts attached to a weighted line. As the crabs were carefully lured near the end of the pier, we would scoop them out of the water with a long-handled net and a happy cry of success from all three children. "He's the biggest one yet!" greeted each crab landing on the pier.

We were also pleased that we were nearing the end of the week with no accidents or illnesses, which is always an accomplishment when three young children are involved.

But now, suddenly and fearfully, our luck was running out. And it was all my fault. I had forgotten to bring a pocket knife to cut the pieces of chicken we tied to the end of our crabbing line, so I took a paring knife from the drawer of the camper's kitchen. After using the knife, I had wiped it clean and carelessly stuck it in the back pocket of my jeans, making a mental note to be very careful with the exposed blade. Mental notes often fail me.

My panicked cry of "No!" was quickly followed by Chris's cry of pain. Dropping the crabbing net and fishing pole I held in my hands, I turned in dread and discovered that the knife had gashed his right leg just above the knee and just below his blue shorts.

Manfully, he insisted that it didn't hurt "too bad" as I picked him up in my arms and rushed to the camper, where we found a first aid kit. We stopped the bleeding as best we could, but it was obvious the cut needed stitches.

"Ewww," Cheryl exclaimed sympathetically, rolling her eyes and turning her head dramatically, as only a 10-year-old sister can, while the rest of us climbed into our Mercury station wagon to seek help at the campground office. The young man in charge gave us directions to the nearest emergency facility, where we waited half an hour before seeing a doctor.

That was 30 minutes longer for me to continue punishing myself for being so careless as to put an open knife in my back pocket and then allowing my son to slide across it while attempting a piggyback ride. What kind of father was I?

My self-recrimination became even more intense as I watched the young, friendly physician place a clean white cloth over the wound with a circular hole just big enough to help him focus on his stitching.

Each stitch wove a portrait of failure on the fabric of my fatherhood. I had always tried to protect my children from harm—even to the point of being accused of being overprotective. Those efforts only exaggerated my present sense of failure.

The physician did a neat job of the stitching, although Chris says he can still see the scar after all these years. Thankfully, however, he never mentions the scars of experiencing his father's failure to protect.

That's the hope of all us imperfect parents, I suppose. We know we make mistakes but fervently hope few lasting scars remain.

I find much hope in the parable of the prodigal son. We are not told what may have occurred in the home to make him want to take his inheritance and simply leave. However, a lot happened to him after he left. The last straw was his competing with hogs for something to eat.

Astoundingly, nothing destroyed his hope of returning home. Of course, he did feel he could only return as a servant and not as a son, but he hadn't reckoned on the unconditional love of his father, who refused to accept him as anything less than a son.

While he was still far off, the father ran and threw his arms around his son, crying out, "Quick! Bring the best robe and put it on him. Put a ring on his finger and sandals on his feet…. Let's have a feast and celebrate. For this son of mine was dead and is alive again; he was lost and is found" (Luke 15:22–24a).

In telling this story, Jesus was presenting the revolutionary idea that God is like a father waiting for his wandering children to return home. And as long as there is a home filled with forgiveness and unconditional love—love that does not have to be earned—there is the possibility that all us prodigal children are never damaged beyond hope.

Many wounds have been stitched and healed with hardly a scar remaining by the experience of unending, unconditional love. So I give thanks that I am not the only father my children have and that the Heavenly Parent loves them even more than I do.

On the way to Mullinix, my personal "home" where I hope to know the Christ more intimately, I try hard not to present exposed knives that may injure my children. But when I fail in those efforts, I trust the unconditional love I learned from our Father-God to help heal their wounds.

A Garden of Gratitude

"I sure hate that Daddy never got to see the crape myrtles bloom," Mother said suddenly, startling me as I sat finishing breakfast while watching her already busy at work on lunch, or "dinner" as we called it in North Carolina.

My mother lived for nine years after my father's death. All of us children thought she would survive one year at the most because my parents had been married for almost 62 years and did everything and went everywhere together. They lived their two lives as one person. Mother spoke often of Daddy after his passing—and we let her—and joined in, because we knew it made him feel more present to her.

One spring day when the crape myrtles were blooming, I had gone down to my hometown of Mt. Gilead, North Carolina, from my home in Williamsburg, Virginia, to visit Mother. I was well aware of her loneliness without Daddy, but until that moment I had failed to realize how sad she was that Daddy never saw the brilliant display of red blossoms along the driveway leading to our home where we had lived from the time I was six years old.

My father had planted the crape myrtles as young saplings after the doctors had told him he had prostate cancer and the prognosis was uncertain. Daddy knew his time was limited, but that never stopped him from planting and looking toward the future.

"Mother," I mumbled through a mouthful of perfectly seasoned, buttered grits, "I don't think Daddy ever expected to see them bloom." When she looked up from the white cook stove and turned toward me, I continued, "I think he planted those crape myrtles for others to enjoy as his way of saying 'thank you' to all those who planted before him."

My father was like that. He was a very optimistic person who saw life as a gift, even the little things that came his way.

About a year before his death, I was sitting at that same breakfast bar separating the kitchen from the dining room when Daddy walked in, setting a black five-gallon bucket stacked high with green beans onto the kitchen floor.

"Well," he said, "that's all the beans we'll get out of the garden this year."

Later that day, roaming the little five-acre homestead past the scuppernong vine on the left and the smokehouse on the right to the falling-down barn beside the lower garden, a walk I would always take on my visits home, I confirmed my father's evaluation. There was absolutely nothing left to harvest. The bean vines had turned brown and were hugging the ground.

But the next morning, as I was sitting down to one of Mother's famous breakfasts of perfectly fried tenderloin, country ham, bacon, sausage, buttered grits, soft scrambled eggs, and fluffy biscuits, my father walked through the back screen door in his white socks after stepping out of the high-top work shoes he always left on the top step of the carport. A ring of morning dew encircled the bottom of both rolled-up jeans legs. That remains one of my favorite images of my father.

There was a twinkle in his eye as he set another five-gallon bucket of green beans on the floor beside the counter where I was eating. "Daddy," I said in surprise, "where did you get those beans? I know there were no more on those dried-up vines in the garden."

He chuckled softly and shook his head with satisfaction as he washed his hands in the kitchen sink to join me for breakfast. I watched him fill his plate at the kitchen stove, hesitating briefly to choose which meat to select. Mother always gave us a choice of meats. I usually chose all of them.

Seeing he had selected the country ham, I said, "Daddy, you can squeeze more out of a garden than anyone I've ever seen." He chuckled again as he walked over to sit beside me at the little bar.

Reflecting on that scene years later, I've concluded that my father could harvest more from a garden than most, partly because of thankfulness. His prostate cancer was not responding well to treatment, and he was so grateful to be out in his beloved garden that he saw things the rest of us failed to notice.

Maybe my father heard Paul's words to the Thessalonians with more understanding than most: "Be joyful always, pray continually, give thanks in all circumstances, for this is God's will for you in Christ Jesus" (1 Thess 5:16–18).

Why "give thanks in all circumstances"? Because right in the middle of this "groaning, decaying" world, there are "first fruits of the Spirit"—"first fruits" of resurrection power that will one day make right what our rebellion against God has made wrong with the whole of creation (Rom 8:23).

One day, it will all be made right, complete and perfect. But in the meantime there are "patches" of resurrection power, episodes of redemption and renewal all around us, clearly obvious to eyes and hearts open to receive because of "giving thanks in all things."

So I believe my father could plant crape myrtles he would never see bloom because thankfulness enabled him to see the "first fruits," keeping him optimistic and hopeful. On the way to Mullinix, I try hard to emulate my father. I try hard, although at times I catch myself replacing gratitude with worry and fail to notice a lot that God is doing all around me.

So I give thanks for grace and forgiveness and renew my journey.

A Last Christmas

My father looked into the mirror, straightened his thick, rounded shoulders, ran his right hand over his thinning hair, and turned to walk slowly toward the voices filled with the excitement of another Christmas morning rising from the living room.

Five years earlier, I had driven down from Williamsburg, Virginia, where I had lived with my family for 30 years, to my hometown of Mt. Gilead, North Carolina, where my parents still lived. I had stayed over until Monday so I could accompany my brother, Kent, and Daddy to the urologist, who had told my father he had prostate cancer.

The news had shaken us all, but we were traveling to Albemarle, a town 18 miles northeast of Mt. Gilead, to see if the doctor had any hopeful options for treatment.

As I climbed out of my Oldsmobile Aurora, a dark premonition stopped me halfway out of the car. I had glanced over at my father as he was exiting my brother's car. We were riding separately since I was heading back to Virginia following the doctor visit.

My daddy's rounded shoulders seemed to be sloping more severely than usual, and his customary smiling face looked grim. But I think it was the stooping shoulders that surrounded me with a growing darkness. Those shoulders had been so strong through the years, carrying our family with strength and grace through the difficulties and trials all families face.

A picture of us three older children clinging to those shoulders as our father carried us to bed, squealing and laughing, flashed into my mind. Like a slideshow, another picture of those shoulders appeared. This time the shoulders were stooping over the living room fireplace, coaxing a blazing fire to life while we watched from the front bedroom where my older sister, Ginny, my younger brother, Kent, and I shared a bed. We watched intently, not daring to grab our school clothes and race to the warmth, where we would hurriedly dress until the fire was roaring up the brick chimney. That fireplace was the only heat in the house and thus the only place we dared dress on a bitterly cold winter morning.

The slideshow of memories continued, and I saw shoulders bending over a bountiful garden, which provided vital vegetables for our small rural family. Then the shoulders were rubbing against the small Guernsey cow at milking time in the growing twilight as my father's skillful hands rapidly sent uninterrupted streams of milk into the silver pail.

Anxiety almost overwhelmed me as I watched those shoulders climb slowly out of Kent's car. Were those strong shoulders nearing their final stretch, finally to be defeated by that dread cancer that brought many strong men to their knees?

That was five years ago, and now my family and I were winding our way carefully down Route 5 from Williamsburg toward Interstate 85 to spend Christmas with my family of origin. The annual Christmas trek was more difficult than usual.

First of all, we were attempting to escape a crippling ice storm that had paralyzed Williamsburg and the surrounding communities. We moved slowly down the winding two-lane road, occasionally stopping so my two sons, Chris and Brian, and I could jump out and move fallen trees that blocked our progress. Even as we grabbed the top end of the trees and pulled them to the side of the road, we kept a sharp eye for falling ice from tall pines that had not yet toppled under the heavy weight of frozen rain.

Our trip was also more difficult than usual because we all knew what awaited us when we arrived at our destination. We had called Mother to let her know when to expect us, and she told us it had been an emotional day for Daddy. He was keenly aware that this would be his last Christmas to gather with family.

And now, on this Christmas morning, it looked as if the weakness and pain from his cancer would keep him in bed, too tired to gather around the family Christmas tree. So I had gone into the bedroom he and Mother had shared for over half a century and said, "Daddy, is there any way you can come in and join us for a few minutes?" I knew it was a selfish request, but I could not bear the thought of our being separated on our father's last Christmas.

So now he was attempting to straighten the shoulders that had lost some of their thickness and take his usual seat by Mother on the couch as the grandchildren distributed the gifts like always. The tree, recently harvested from a nearby field by my brother, also looked like it always did with its limp limbs drooping under the weight of decorations, which were older than the grandchildren.

We tried to make Christmas as much like usual as we could, but my father's gifts were very different, and my heart sank as he opened each one: pajamas, slippers, robes—gifts for dying. Not the usual tools and work clothes and Mennen aftershave lotion, gifts for living. I found the change deeply depressing.

A couple months later, during the second week of February, my family called to say that hospice had been called in and Daddy didn't have long to live. I came down to help care for him and give a short respite to family members who were all exhausted from tending to our father day and night.

One early morning, just after midnight, I crawled into Daddy's bed to rest a little and lie on the covers beside him. As I closed my eyes, I sensed movement and saw my father's hand reaching upward toward something or someone he could see clearly but I could only imagine.

The next day I tried to describe the experience:

Closing my fatigued eyes for a moment's rest,
I felt you move and watched as your hand
Reached for an elusive reality in the
        unreal world of pain and narcotics.
Your terror-stricken eyes fought to make
        sense of that shadowy valley lying
                between life and death.
I remembered a small boy in this same room
        in the middle of a black night
Seeing a thousand terrors in his childish
                imaginations.
You reached toward my pallet on the
        floor and covered my small trembling
                hand
And held it in the darkness 'til the demons
        were chased and sleep came.
Remembering, I reach up and place my hand
        over your pale, trembling hand
And, lowering it gently to the bed, hold it
        tightly until your eyes close in peaceful
                sleep.
Thank you for the chance to bring love full
                circle.

I lay beside my father, wide awake, reflecting on the verse that reads, "We love because he first loved us" (1 John 4:19). I thought how that, in addition to God's love giving us the power and the motivation to love, loving God and others is really our opportunity to return the love he has lavished on us. Somehow that makes the act of loving even more satisfying for me.

But perhaps most comforting of all, the circle of receiving and returning love surrounds me with the feel of eternity.

As the minutes and hours slowly passed, accompanied by Daddy's increasingly shallow breathing, I was filled with the urgency, as I make my way toward Mullinix, to return love while there is still time.

Part Five

Church Life

Foolishness in Need of Grace

On November 1, 2015, I broke a perfect streak of 48 years. I toppled a stack of bread plates while leading a service of Communion. I had heard stories of pastors dropping plates and trays, but I had never personally experienced the loud clatter and sudden embarrassment of such a mishap.

The worship service in the church where I had served as an interim pastor a few years back was moving along smoothly when one of the deacons handed me a note. I have always prided myself on my ability to focus on the immediate task before me no matter what is happening around me. But the note was handed to me by the only woman deacon just as I was placing the fourth bread tray on top of the three already stacked on the left side of the Communion table where I was standing.

You may be wondering why I didn't just ignore the note and simply place it in my pocket to read later. I did that once, and it did not turn out well.

We were enjoying a church dinner back in the late 1980s when a close friend and loyal supporter, Marge O'Shell, handed me a note, looked straight into my eyes, and said emphatically, "Read this." Well, I fully intended to since I always found it wise to follow Marge's instructions. But I was in the middle of a conversation with two other parishioners and stuck the note in my shirt pocket to read later.

Later turned out to be that evening when I was removing my shirt in preparation for bed. Suddenly, I remembered the note. My heart rate reached a dangerous level, and my blood pressure zoomed upward as I sat down heavily on the foot of the bed after reading what Marge had written: "Your fly is open."

Collapsing back onto the bed, I stared at the ceiling and began rehearsing the events of the evening: led prayer meeting at floor level with no pulpit to protect my modesty from the eyes of approximately 75 prayer warriors; had conversations with dozens of people before and after the fellowship dinner; and finally stood at the door saying goodbye to visitors and members who, on reflection, did seem a bit too amused to have just heard a list of heavy prayer requests.

As a young pastor I had heard that Dr. Carl Bates, one of our leading Baptists at the time, purportedly told about the time one of his sweet, elderly parishioners asked him, "Dr. Bates, what's the last thing you do before you walk into the pulpit?" Not wanting to lie or maybe wanting to punch a little hole in her too-syrupy piety, Dr. Bates replied, "Ma'am, the last thing I do before walking into the pulpit is check my fly."

I didn't know whether that story was true or not, but after hearing it, I made a lifelong practice of following the example of that great leader and preacher. But finally, I had failed to follow my habitual routine, and one of my worst nightmares—close behind every pastor's recurring nightmare of forgetting my scripture and every point of the sermon while a church full of people sit looking at me expectantly as I flip frantically through my Bible—had struck with alarming consequences.

Now, here I was again, leading another service from floor level with another well-intentioned friend handing me a note, whispering for me to "read it." I knew immediately what I had to do.

Holding the note in my left hand, I tried to sneak a peek when I realized the writing was so small that I needed my glasses, which, of course, were in my jacket pocket. All of this was happening while I was placing the fourth bread tray on the stack of three already in place. My usually reliable focus was completely destroyed, and my left hand, holding both the note and the last tray, bumped the stack of trays and toppled them toward the floor with an irreverent clatter.

Several of the nearest deacons lunged heroically toward the falling trays. We did save most of them from falling onto the floor, but looking down, I saw little pieces of Jesus' symbolic body scattered around my feet. The only thing left to do was try to avoid stepping on the bread and feeling even more of an infidel than I already did.

While the deacons were distributing the Welch's grape juice, I was finally able to take out my glasses and read the note, which turned out to be a relatively inconsequential announcement the woman deacon wanted me to make at the conclusion of the service. No open fly. Nothing smeared on my face. Nothing worthy of my losing focus on the task at hand. Just an announcement, which after all that transpired, I forgot to make anyway.

Following the benediction, I was hurrying down the aisle, bracing myself for the inevitable kidding at the front door by well-meaning people who did not realize I had just broken a 48-year streak of perfectly executed Lord's Suppers.

Suddenly, a man with whom I had watched numerous ballgames in his man cave (a converted detached garage), stepped out into the aisle, halting my progress, put his arm around me, and whispered, "Pastor, I don't care if you did fumble. You can be on my team any time."

Those few words immediately transformed my sense of abject failure into a healing experience of grace. After all, that's what the supper we had just celebrated is all about: Our Lord giving his all that we might be forgiven for all our failures far beyond all our deserving.

On the way to Mullinix, that symbolic place where I allow God's kingdom to truly abide in me, I need small acts of grace from fellow travelers to remind me of God's infinite grace. Small acts of sudden, unexpected grace, like the one from my friend, which remind me that God has a passion to transform all my failure and fumbling foolishness into renewed strength and wholeness.

In fact, Paul assures the Corinthian Christians that "God has chosen the foolish things of the world to shame the wise. God chose the weak things of the world to shame the strong" (1 Cor 1:27).

I like to think that things like leading a prayer meeting with an open fly and dropping Communion plates for the first time in 48 years are covered by that assurance.

Going to Mullinix

Living Each Day to the Fullest

L ife is filled with mystery. I will never understand this.

As she quietly, almost imperceptibly, slipped into a coma, all the phones refused to ring. All night long and throughout the next day as she lay in that unconscious state, the grandfather clock standing at the end of the couch, which had become her bed in her final days, did not strike.

On the first quarter hour, after she had breathed her last in this world and had taken her first step into the next, the clock began chiming.

I paused to pinch both legs and slap my face harder than I had intended as I slipped into the driver's seat of my little Chevrolet Corsica. When I arrived back at my church study, I called her best friend who had not left her side for two weeks and asked, "Did that really happen? I pinched both legs and slapped myself hard, and it hurt, so I think I was awake."

Chuckling easily, as if she were indulging the innocent questions of a small child, the friend replied, "It happened. She was a special person, and I would expect her transition from this world to the next to be exceptional." She paused a minute before continuing. "By the way, the phone started ringing again right after you left."

We talked for a while before she signed off with these words, "But you're the theologian. I'll leave it up to you to explain."

This extraordinary woman, whom I'll call Irene, had called me six years prior to ask if she could stop by the church on the way home from her doctor because she needed my help in breaking the doctor's diagnosis of terminal cancer to her family. We came up with a plan and relayed the difficult news as gently as we could. I stayed very close to Irene and her family during the next few years.

Now, six years later, on a late Monday morning, Irene called again, and again she had just left her oncologist's office. He had told her she had around two weeks to live.

"I'm okay," she said confidently. "I'm in God's care. But I'm worried about my husband and three boys. I need you to help me tell them that what they've been dreading for several years is getting close."

We agreed that I would come to their home the next day, late Tuesday afternoon, when things were quietest. Irene met me at the front door with a plan. "I want you to tell my family what the doctor said, and then I have some things to say." So we did it that way.

After they had a few moments to absorb the doctor's news, which I quietly relayed, Irene said with tender love but no hint of sentimentality, "I know this is hard, but sooner or later this comes to every family. There is a time for everything, and this is our time."

She paused a moment to gather her thoughts before continuing. "I'm okay. God is going to take care of me. I just want to make sure that each of you continues to go on with your daily lives. I want you to live each day to the fullest."

Her husband, whom I'll call Bob, had a Lion's Club meeting scheduled for that night. Bowing his head and fighting tears, he said, "I'm staying home."

Irene immediately responded, "Bob, look at me. You didn't hear me. I said I want you and the boys to go on with your lives and live each day to the fullest." Bob went to his Lion's Club meeting.

The next afternoon, I returned to Irene's home, wondering on the way why she chose those particular words for her family: "Live each day to the fullest." Over the years I had heard family members share many "last words" but never with that particular phraseology.

Taking my seat on the couch/bed next to Irene, I noticed several books scattered on the coffee table in front of the couch. One in particular caught my eye. It was titled simply Carpe Diem, which I immediately recognized as the well-known Latin phrase meaning "seize the day."

It was the subtitle, however, that really intrigued me: Enjoying Every Day with a Terminal Illness. My first reaction was irritation at the seemingly breezy presumption of such a subtitle. I had suffered with many families in which one member had a terminal illness. It was not fun—for any of us.

I discovered, however, that the author, Ed Madden, a former chemistry teacher turned journalist, did indeed have a right to write that book since he also had a terminal illness.

As I thumbed through the book, Irene told me what it had meant to her. "It opened my eyes to what is going on around me each day, each moment," she said. "And I'm determined not to miss any of it in the days I have left." She paused and looked at two family pictures on the wall before continuing, "Neither do I want my illness and death to cause my family to miss the richness of life each day."

Going to Mullinix

Irene then told me how the book had led her to a passage in Matthew: "So do not worry about tomorrow, for tomorrow will bring worries of its own. Today's trouble is enough for today" (Matt 6:34).

"And that," Irene said, "is when I stopped worrying about what my cancer would do to me tomorrow and started focusing on what God is doing today."

Irene explained how that new perspective awakened her to the loving people around her every day, to how God's creation reflected his presence, how little things said big things to her: the laughter of neighborhood children playing in their backyards, the singing of birds on dripping tree branches after a sudden shower, and so many other little things she had failed to notice became signs of God's nearness and care.

Near the end of our visit that day, Irene asked thoughtfully, "Does it always take a terminal illness to wake us up to life?"

"I guess each individual has to answer that question for himself or herself," I said.

I'm still working on answering that question for myself. And that other question? Why the phones stopped ringing and the clock chimes were silent during the last 24 hours of Irene's life?

If I looked hard enough, I might find logical explanations. But I have no trouble accepting mystery in the spiritual realm. In fact, I would worry if there were no mystery. A lack of mystery would mean I am limiting God to the boundaries of my own knowledge and understanding—cutting God down to my size in order to make sense of everything.

So I don't really need to explain what caused the silence of the phones and the stoppage of the clock.

I'll tell you what I like to imagine. I like to think that Irene's faithful focus on the present moment was so powerful that it suspended the passing of time in her little piece of the world for just a few hours.

There was no yesterday. No tomorrow. Only this present time and the hovering silence of God's tender care, too dense to be penetrated by the sounds of a ringing phone or a chiming clock.

The multiplication of mysteries along the way is perhaps a sign that I am drawing nearer to Mullinix. Maybe the complete oneness with God that I seek will come more quickly as I eagerly accept his exalted "otherness."

Thank you, Irene.

Overexpecting?

He walked into my study on the second day of January 1997. His tense face and slumped shoulders painted an unmistakable portrait of a troubled man. He had reason to be troubled.

Through a number of personal bad decisions and several malevolent decisions of others, my friend was in a very difficult situation. For an hour and a half we explored potential actions and their likely consequences.

Finally, growing exhausted after so much mental wrestling, he stood to leave. Shaking my hand warmly and forcing a smile, he said, "Well, Pastor, I'm going to anticipate the best."

I still admire his attitude, but as soon as he had left, I asked myself, "Does he have the right to anticipate the best? He's in a mighty messy situation. Does he have a sound foundation on which to base that kind of optimism, or is it just so much futile wishful thinking?"

I was accused one time by someone who didn't know me very well (or maybe knew me too well) that I might be a touch too skeptical for a pastor. I admit that I have never been blindly optimistic. In some folks' minds, unbridled optimism is a primary qualification for people of the cloth. I think I am basically an optimistic person, but I do need something on which to base my optimism.

Consequently, I guard against overexpecting. I want to live "anticipating the best," but at the same time I don't want to overexpect and suffer the frustration, discouragement, and even depression that wait in the shadows to pounce on expectations that are unrealistic and have no hope of materializing.

I've been there and done that.

I had high expectations on that morning in 1986 over in Huddleston, Virginia. I was preaching at a revival for longtime friends Lytle and Suzanne Buckingham, strong members of our church during their student days at the College of William and Mary in the early to mid-70s. Both were instrumental in helping us begin an effective ministry to college students.

I decided to arise early on the first morning of the weeklong revival to work out in their basement gymnasium next to my guest bedroom. At 45 years of age, I was saying things like old Caleb said 45 years after he insisted the children of Israel could take the promised land from the "giants."

Forty-five years after that, Caleb declared, "I am as good as I was [then].... I am as strong to this day as I was in the day that Moses sent me to spy out the land" (Josh 14:11). Confident, boastful, prideful words. That kind of arrogance seems to have become the norm in modern times.

I was certainly full of self-assurance on that morning as I lay on the weight bench and grabbed the bar over my head without bothering to count the multiple weights on each end. After all, "I am as strong as I ever was."

But after a few quick, short, confident repetitions, I found myself lying helplessly under the weight bar, which was now pressing painfully against my chest. Lifting the bar with all my fast-flagging strength, I failed to move it more than two inches above my heaving torso.

Panic set in, along with weighty questions such as "when does a person cross the line between optimism and reality; robust faith and fantasy; realistic expectations and overexpectations?" (In case you've ever wondered what clergy do during times of extreme crises, we often ask such deep theological questions.)

I knew I had definitely crossed some kind of line. I estimated it would be another hour before the Buckinghams began stirring for breakfast. What to do? Should I call out and suffer the humiliation of being found like this? Rationalizing my silence, I wondered what it would do to the budding faith of the two young children, Nancy and Jimmy, to see the helpless squirming of a pitifully pinned preacher.

Resuming my efforts to lift the bar, I suddenly realized that with each futile attempt, the bar was inching closer and closer to my throat and certain death by suffocation. I could imagine the headline in our local newspaper, The Virginia Gazette: "Pastor Suffocated by Pride." I've seen that happen.

Growing desperate, I took a quick inventory of those body parts I could risk damaging with the least amount of lasting consequences. Making my decision, I began lowering one end of the bar toward the floor. Halfway through this process, the searing pain made me question if I had chosen the right body parts to risk injuring.

The bar and weights finally fell to the floor with a bang loud enough to wake the entire household—which it did. Lytle and Jimmy suddenly appeared at the door with a cheerful greeting: "Getting in an early morning workout?" Grunting in reply, I hastily reached for a five-pound barbell with my left hand and began curling it painfully.

"Join me?" I asked, praying that they would assume my breathlessness was from exertion rather than searing pain. Evidently they did, and I didn't tell them what had happened until years later.

But I did tell our building planning committee when I returned to Williamsburg. Our church was wrestling with a decision on whether to build a large new sanctuary or expand our original little L-shaped multipurpose structure.

Some of us in our still fairly small congregation were certain that we were overexpecting if we went ahead with sanctuary plans. We would never be able to meet those weighty mortgage payments. They would press down on us until they threatened our very existence through financial suffocation.

Tom Campbell, chairman of our building planning committee, drew a caricature of my experience with the weights, titling it "We Must Avoid Overexpectations."

But a short few months later, we broke ground on a new sanctuary. What happened? We became convinced that it was God's will that we build. We also became convinced that "with man this is impossible, but with God all things are possible" (Matt 19:26).

On that early morning in 1986, I lay squirming as helpless as a worm because I expected too much of myself and my own limited strength. I didn't even wait for a "spotter." When we trust ourselves too much and God too little, we always tend to overexpect.

I guess that means if I am to reach Mullinix, my symbol of mature kingdom living, I must cease walking the paths I choose and recommit to the road fresh with the footprints of the One I am following.

"Going to Mullinix," then, becomes a journey on tiptoes with "eager expectation" of what God has in store for his creation: liberation "from its bondage to decay and brought into the glorious freedom of the children of God" (Rom 8:21).

Somehow, I don't think I can ever overexpect when God is involved.

Attacked in a Grocery Store

Pastors are not immune to becoming ensnared in the sticky tentacles of a midlife crisis. I wasn't bothered when I hit the half-century mark or even reached 60 years of age, but turning 40 bothered me, and I was restless to make a change.

The options for change are limited for a pastor. I couldn't afford a Carolina blue convertible like one of my parishioners who came home with a sporty Chrysler on the day of his 40th birthday. His wife enjoyed calling it her husband's "midlife Chrysler."

I couldn't afford a new car, and I didn't want to change churches or wives since I loved them both. So I was quickly discarding most of the changes some men choose when entering the midlife years.

Around the time those octopus-like tentacles of midlife were sucking me into a crisis, I took a trip with the senior members of our church in a van that had an unusually high step leading into the cab area. Helping one of the elderly women negotiate that step, she and I simultaneously noticed that her rather snug dress moved well above her knees when she lifted her foot onto the first step.

She was obviously deeply embarrassed and turned to apologize to her pastor for showing so much leg. In an effort to cover her humiliation, I quickly said, "Don't worry about it, Liz. My weakness is liquor."

Liz began laughing so uncontrollably that it took a while for both of us to stagger into the van and find our seats. Until her death many years later, Liz often reminded me of that day, and we always had a good laugh. But I knew not many of our good church folk would be laughing if my midlife crisis turned in the direction of women, wine, and song.

So with such limited options, I grew a beard. I know that seems quite harmless, but this was back before anyone, especially clergy, started growing facial hair, and a few people weren't very happy that I was bucking their image of an ideal pastor. Most, however, accepted the black beard with just a little good-natured kidding about "hiding that pretty face."

As silly as it seems to me now, the beard was enough to quell my restless desire for some change to carry me through the realization that I was no longer a young man but had crossed over into adulthood, that precarious minefield of increased expectations. No longer could my foibles be excused with, "Well, he's still young."

During the following years, that full, black beard only caused one serious problem—it made me much more recognizable. At the time, I was the only pastor in the little village of Williamsburg, Virginia, with a beard. By the way, I was also the first pastor in town to wear colored shirts in the pulpit, which also caused a minor stir among our more traditional members. (Most of my rebellions have been small.)

However, our loving people were very tolerant and understanding of the frailties of their pastor during his silly struggles to enter the world of adulthood. I tried to love them all unconditionally, but such understanding on their part made it easier.

Around the time of my minor midlife crisis, we were attempting to meet one of the needs in our community by establishing, in partnership with Riverside Health Systems, an adult daycare center in our fellowship hall. As part of the process, we had to go before the city council or some sort of judicial body for a hearing that was open to the public.

The public turned out to be most of our neighbors.

Seems they were concerned with what an influx of old people would do to the neighborhood. "Suppose they get loose and start walking through our yards," some argued. It was interesting to me that the majority of those protesting were as old, or older, than those potential clients of our adult daycare. We tried to assure them that our security measures would guard against any clients "escaping."

But it was a change, and any kind of change seems to strike fear in the hearts of most. Approval for the adult daycare, which would care for senior members of families while both their caregivers worked, was in jeopardy because of all the objections from neighbors. We persisted since we felt it was a worthy ministry, keeping many at home, delaying their move to an assisted-living facility or nursing home.

After a long period of heated debate, the application passed by a slim majority. I've noticed, during my now seven decades of observing the human species, that vested interests always fight a ferocious battle against altruistic proposals. Seems most folks want a better world but not if it inconveniences them any.

Some of our neighbors remained upset long after the local government's approval, and as I said, my beard made me easily recognizable as the leader of that church on Jamestown Road initiating all sorts of subversive movements. So one afternoon while I was shopping at Food Lion in the Williamsburg Shopping Center and reaching for a jar of smooth Peter Pan peanut butter on aisle six next to the jellies, I felt a hot breath on the back of my neck.

I turned so quickly that I bumped shoulders with a stooped, red-faced, gray-haired woman who under most circumstances would have looked distinguished but was finding it difficult to pull that off with a deep crimson face spitting vitriolic words in my direction, six inches from my suddenly pale face.

I stood quietly, holding tightly to my medium-size jar of smooth Peter Pan peanut butter, completely cowed by the ferocity of this diminutive woman's attack. I was startled because, up to that moment, I had always considered grocery stores one of the "safe zones."

"You're the pastor of that church that wants to bring all those old people into our neighborhood, aren't you?" I knew I should have shaved and become anonymous after that public hearing.

"Yes, ma'am, I guess so," I stammered, holding my tongue firmly between my teeth so as not to tell her that I didn't expect anyone to enroll older than she looked.

"What are we going to do when those dementia-challenged people start walking across our yards, stepping on our daffodils and tulips and roses and marigolds, and, and…"

She was momentarily running out of flowers, so I took that opportunity to say, "I'm sorry you feel that way. We were only trying to meet a need for you ol'… those older citizens of our community."

While she was shaking her white head furiously and sputtering, evidently still trying to recall more of the flowers in her yard, I said, "'Scuse me, ma'am," and rushed toward the checkout line, beating her by a good 20 feet even though she was exceptionally quick for a 90-year-old.

Most of the time, it was a joy to be recognized as the pastor of Walnut Hills Baptist Church. So I kept my beard. I loved being pastor of a family of good, faithful people who kept trying to love God and love their neighbors by meeting community needs in a variety of creative ways in spite of numerous challenges and obstacles.

That gives me some hope of getting close to my destination of Mullinix, that place of full kingdom living, in spite of all the detours and spiritual roadblocks I encounter. This verse also gives me encouragement: "When they saw the courage of Peter and John and realized that they were unschooled, ordinary men, they were astonished and they took note that these men had been with Jesus" (Acts 4:13).

Ordinary men who looked like Jesus.

Such words open wider the possibility that, ordinary as I am, I can become recognizable as a follower of Jesus.

I still have my beard, but somehow I don't think that will help me look more like Jesus.

Shotgun Christians

A submersible baptistery heater has the potential for spawning dramatic events such as the one that occurred on a cold February morning in 1984.

Our first baptistery in our first little L-shaped building that served as our worship, fellowship, and Sunday school areas for 18 years had such a heater. A ladder, which shivered slightly as the baptismal candidates climbed to the top, was a challenge for some of our older, larger members.

You had to be serious about your desire to be baptized to climb that ladder. Therefore, it was a good, straightforward test of sincerity.

The biggest challenge with a submersible heater, however, was achieving the right water temperature. Our first heater warmed the water quite adequately— assuming it was operating correctly. A float attached to a long rod turned the heater on when it was lifted by the rising water and shut the heater off when the water level dropped. That bit of engineering served us well until the baptistery sprang a slight leak during one freezing February night, dropping the water level until the bobbing float disengaged the heater.

When Roger Higgs, the chairman of our baptistery committee, arrived early that Sunday morning to make final preparations for the service, not only was there not enough water to dunk a baby, which we were theologically opposed to anyway, but the small amount of water that remained was as cold as February water straight out of the tap. Which, of course, it was.

For two hours Roger hauled buckets of hot water from the men's bathroom just outside the double-door entrance to our worship/fellowship/Sunday school room. The odds were stacked against Roger since at the same time he was emptying buckets of hot water into the baptistery, it was necessary to run the cold water from the tap into the tank in order to reach a depth sufficient for a proper Baptist baptism.

We Baptists require a lot of water in our attempt to be theologically correct, as we understand it. After all, John the Baptist had the entire Jordan River at his disposal when he baptized Jesus. February was a little cold to plunge into the James River, but we still wanted a sufficient amount of water to get everyone soaking wet.

Quite a battle raged between Roger's buckets of hot water and the cold tap water. The cold water won.

The music and scripture and sermon all focused on the sacrament of baptism, but I gave the candidates, three adults and four older children, the choice of postponing to another time. The vote was unanimous: "Some of our families have come a long way to be here with us. Let's go!"

When I stepped into the water in my high-top waders, I wished I had cast a decisive "no!" vote. My feet became numb almost immediately, and I worried about losing my balance and diving on top of the candidates as I lowered them into the water while standing on two frozen nubs.

The younger, more hearty candidates, were first to be baptized, and apart from some visible trembling of purple lips and the involuntary chattering of teeth, things proceeded uneventfully.

But now it was time for the grownups, who, like me, can be pretty wimpy in the presence of cold water. Just as I had expected, when the first young woman in her late 20s stepped into the icy water, a loud gasp, audible all the way to the back pew, escaped her lips.

A small titter of laughter rolled through the congregation. As each one of the adults stepped into the water, the gasps grew louder, and laughter now flowed freely down every pew.

Nevertheless, we pressed on until now we were down to the last candidate, a lovely woman in her mid-60s who had chronic respiratory problems. I leaned toward her as she stood poised precariously on the top step of the ladder and whispered, "Mary, are you sure you want to go ahead with this? I don't want it to make you ill."

Nodding emphatically for me to proceed, she stepped over the edge of the baptistery and onto the first step leading into the tub. Mary's eyes grew wider and wider as the water rose higher and higher up her baptismal robe. A look of terror filled her face as she took her place in front of me.

I held both her hands tightly in my right hand and placed my left hand behind her neck, preparing to lower her backward into the water with my usual words from the apostle Paul: "We were therefore buried with him through baptism into death" (Rom 6:4). I prayed fervently that I was still referring to a spiritual death and not a literal death.

Mary's eyes rolled back into her head as she braced herself for the icy plunge. My relief was palpable as I lifted her from the water and watched her walk unsteadily up the steps of the baptistery and disappear over the edge.

On Monday morning as I walked into my study, my secretary told me that Mary was calling on line two. Uttering a quick prayer, I picked up the phone and said with more cheer than I was feeling, "Good morning, Mary. Are you calling from the hospital?"

"No," she replied, laughing. "As a matter of fact, I feel great."

"You do?" I stammered in surprise.

"Pastor," she continued, "I feel so much more optimistic about my chances of making it through the pearly gates than ever."

"I don't understand," I replied, genuinely puzzled. I had always made sure that people understood that it was their faith and not the act of baptism that saved them.

Laughter filled her voice as she explained, "Oh, don't worry. I understood what you said about faith and grace." She paused before continuing. "But when you plunged me under that icy water, it scared whatever part of the devil was left in me, clean out!"

Hanging up the phone with a chuckle and profound relief, I found myself reflecting on a question I have never answered to my satisfaction: "What is the place of fear in our coming to the Christ?" Of course, I knew Mary was joking about the devil being scared out of her. But for much of my ministry, that has been a serious concern: "Can the devil really be scared out of a person?"

I have always felt that the strongest relationship with Jesus is forged through responding to the drawing power of God's gift of love in his Son. After all, Jesus said, "But I, when I am lifted up from the earth, will draw all men to myself" (John 12:32).

So my primary approach to evangelism has been to emphasize "for God so loved the world that he gave his only Son" (John 3:16) and trust the power of that love to draw people into a personal relationship. But sometimes I wonder if I should have warned people more about the consequences of failing to believe and refusing to accept the loving grace of the Redeemer-Christ.

So I've asked questions. Can authentic love really result from an individual being scared to the altar? Is it possible for a couple to fall in love following a shotgun wedding? Can a "shotgun Christian" fall in love with Jesus? Have I been too reluctant to accept the reality of faith that is born in a foxhole? Does such faith endure the test of time, or does it merely last until the person crawls out of the foxhole?

Such questions began early in life. I can even pinpoint the day. Our family had attended a night of revival meetings in a neighboring church, Holly Mount Baptist Church. The visiting evangelist was gifted at stirring up fear and even terror. This was somewhere close to the beginning of the Cold War.

I had been baptized the summer before and felt secure about my eternal destination—until that night. The evangelist painted graphic pictures of what would happen to America in light of the Communist threat unless we "turned to the Lord."

His most gruesome picture was of Russian soldiers throwing infants into the air to catch them on the points of their swords. I could not imagine a more horrible scene. Lots of young mothers couldn't either as, weeping profusely, they dragged their babies and small children down the aisle to "give their hearts to Jesus."

I could feel the sweat on my own forehead and was keenly aware that my antiperspirant had lost its valiant struggle with "fear sweat" halfway through that frightening sermon.

Standing off to the side as the pastor received the new converts, the visiting evangelist bowed his head with a satisfied, beatific smile. He was well aware of how good he was at eliciting decisions. This scene repeated itself every time on the last night of his weeklong August revivals following an emotional, dramatic invitation.

The back seat of our old Dodge, where we three children rode and argued and wrestled, was unusually quiet on the way home, each of us afraid to speak. We weren't sure what the future or the surrounding darkness held or if the devil himself was riding in the back seat with us. That evangelist was good.

Then my father spoke quietly as if reflecting to himself, almost unaware he was speaking aloud. "I wonder if fear is the best way to bring people to faith. I don't remember hearing a word tonight about God's love." My father was a very independent thinker and never accepted anything at face value.

Those few words were all I remember him ever saying on the subject of fear and faith. He was a man of few words, but as usual, those few words had a profound effect on me.

That was the time and place my questions about the place of fear in faith began, questions that have sometimes kept me awake at night. I have talked often about Bonhoeffer's emphasis on the "cost of discipleship." But was I talking enough about Dallas Willard's emphasis on the "cost of non-discipleship," which he explores in a number of his books on spiritual formation?

Finally, after a period of restless squirming in my study chair, following Mary's phone call, I reminded myself to trust God's grace in forgiving my inadequacies and covering my mistakes, even the ones I was never quite sure I had made. It always does come down to grace, reluctant as I am to forgive my own imperfections.

I guess it also comes down to the truth that the risen Christ can find many ways to bring people to himself. I trust that to mean he can also use many avenues to draw me nearer my Mullinix destination and the love and understanding that characterize mature kingdom citizens.

A Wedding Tornado

The young couple, married just five hours earlier, had finally retired for their overnight stay at the historic inn before embarking on their weeklong honeymoon. Suddenly, they were startled by an urgent knocking on their bedroom door and a voice crying out, "You have to leave immediately!"

"Who is that?" the bride asked, puzzled.

"Sounds like your mother," an equally bewildered groom replied as the knocking persisted and the voice cried out again, "Can you hear me? You have to leave this room immediately!"

Thirty minutes earlier, the cellphone in the left front pocket of my navy blue suit pants—recently splattered with melted wax from the votives I had hurriedly helped my florist wife collect—began vibrating insistently against my leg as I exited slowly down the dirt drive of the old inn.

I was happy everything had gone so well. The threat of rain had dissipated just in time for us to move the inside preparations outside, which was good for the wedding but difficult for my wife and those of us assisting her to change sites in time for the ceremony.

We met the 5:00 p.m. deadline by eight minutes, even though I had to officiate in a perspiration-soaked shirt with, thankfully, only one small sweat spot seeping through the left front panel of my once-stylish three-buttoned suit jacket. Fortunately, all that water did not short-circuit the microphone hanging over my left ear.

I should know after officiating approximately 400 weddings not to stress over such things as deadlines and stifling heat. I haven't failed yet to complete the uniting in marriage of bride and groom, no matter how many unexpected challenges occur. I tell that to panicky brides all the time. I still have a little trouble convincing myself.

I waited off to the side with the handsome groom, who was nervously shifting from foot to foot under the shade of a massive old oak tree that no doubt had overseen almost as many weddings as I had performed in over 45 years as a pastor. I waited, thinking my tired legs were telling me I was getting too old for this double involvement of assisting my wife decorate as an unskilled errand boy and then quickly redirecting my focus to providing a warm, personal, ordered, seamless ceremony suitable for videotaping and replaying for all the relatives at every anniversary and family reunion.

As I stood waiting for the signal from the wedding coordinator to begin, I was also questioning my judgment at playing racquetball earlier that morning, knowing how full and lengthy the day was going to be. Perhaps my weary legs were an indication of a lack of intelligence as much as a lack of youth. Nevertheless, I'm fiercely fighting the aging process at every ache of my muscles and joints and every new stiffness in my neck and back. I intend to go down swinging.

But I was grateful that everything, including the reception, had proceeded smoothly. Of course, during the concluding dance, the disc jockey had asked couples to exit the dance floor according to the number of years they had been married.

As usual, having been married for 52 years, Jean and I stood alone after all the other couples had, one by one, shuffled off the dance floor. The prize for winning this game is always the same: being asked by the disc jockey what advice we had for the newly married in order for them to enjoy a long marriage.

"Well," I replied quickly, "first of all, you have to stay alive for many years. Longevity is the key."

My wife, not at all amused, hurriedly interrupted. After all these years, our sense of humor is still not fully aligned. "Overlook their faults and love them anyway," she said pointedly, glancing in my direction.

I should have anticipated that since I had been a little hard to live with during the last couple extremely stressful weeks. I quickly added a therapeutic fishing trip to my mental list of things to do the following week.

The disc jockey looked at me and said with a chuckle, "Do you have anything more to add?"

I felt the pressure to step up, so I said, "Call out and celebrate the good qualities of your spouse," thinking that might win back a few points I had obviously recently lost. My wife did seem to be duly impressed.

The cellphone vibrating against my leg kept demanding attention, so I reluctantly pulled it out of my pocket. Startled, I read an emergency alert: "A tornado has been spotted in your area. Take shelter immediately."

Backing into a turnaround, I returned to the reception area and urgently informed everyone about the warning. The family and guests who were still present seemed concerned, but since there seemed to be no immediate danger, we all continued assisting in the cleanup.

Angela, or rather "Lulu," my sister-in-law who was visiting us from Atlanta in order to help with the wedding, came in after a trip to her van and said, "It feels real strange out there, so still." A moment later, the roar of a fast-moving wind reached our ears, accompanied by a fiercely pounding rain.

"Run for the basement!" the owner of the wedding venue shouted. Grabbing each other by arms and hands and flapping pieces of already-drenched clothing, we fought the wind pushing against us at each step. I saw my wife being pulled along by the young wedding coordinator up ahead as she shouted encouragingly, "You can make it, Miss Jean! You can make it!"

Assured they were making as much progress as I was with the bride's father's hand firmly grasping my right elbow, I glanced up at the wildly twisting limbs of the ancient trees, wondering which one, each the size of small trees, would be the first to crash down on us.

By great good fortune we made it to safety and rushed through the basement door, clutched firmly in the hands of a large man, imploring us to hurry. "Come on! Come on!" he shouted while furiously waving us down the steps.

As we gathered in excited but relieved huddles, a voice shouted, "Check to make sure your family and friends made it!"

Names of those who were not immediately spotted were called out. All answered from various corners of the basement just as the electricity failed and we were plunged into darkness so deep the face of the person next to us instantly vanished.

"Don't worry," the large man holding the door earlier called out. "The generator will switch on in a moment." It did but also cut off two or three times before remaining on, adding to the strange, eerie feel of the night.

About that time, in the middle of all that chaos, the bride's mother remembered that her daughter and new husband had retired to their room upstairs. Upstairs was not a safe place in the middle of this storm. Racing up the basement steps, she knocked loudly on their door.

After a few moments of hurried explanation, the new husband and wife trudged down the stairs to the basement and had the pleasure of spending the first hour and a half of their wedding night sitting on a concrete floor with their rain-drenched family and guests talking about the weather.

They seemed a little disappointed.

From my hard seat on the floor, I idly wondered how many of the couples I had married over approximately half a century began their wedding night with a frantic mother knocking on their bedroom door telling them they had to quit whatever they were doing and leave immediately.

I guessed the percentage was pretty low.

After an hour and a half in the basement, drying out and conversing in subdued tones, I told my wife and sister-in-law, "Sounds like the storm is dying down a little. Let's see if we can make it home."

Driving around and sometimes over small trees and large limbs that had been effortlessly tossed onto the road by the powerful wind and straining to see through the heavy, dark rain, we managed to stay approximately within the lines of Interstate 64 for 24 miles, arriving at our home in Williamsburg near midnight, exhausted but thankful.

Lying in bed later that night, my aching body too tired and too charged with adrenaline to sleep, that unpleasant thought forced itself back into my mind: "I'm getting too old for this." Just as quickly, however, another thought rushed in.

The father of the groom, a deeply religious man who cared greatly that his son experience a strong beginning in his matrimonial adventure, had engaged me in a lengthy conversation earlier in the evening concerning my pre- and post-marital counseling. He seemed satisfied.

Approaching me again following the ceremony, the groom's father thanked me for my words. Then, staring at me intently, he said, "I think you were put on this earth just for this moment."

It would be impossible to count the number of moments in a life spanning over 75 years, moments in which decisions were made and actions were taken that affected my life and the lives of many others. So to hear that this was the moment for which I had been put on the earth was startling.

But I suppose there are many moments that help define our reason for taking up space on this overcrowded, spinning orb. However, to crawl into bed with the hope that, no matter at what age, the next moment of my life holds the potential of fulfilling my destiny brought a peaceful close to a frenetic day.

While the thunder still rumbled in the distance and I slipped into the first vestiges of light sleep, a quiet assurance flowed through my soul: "The floods came, and the winds blew, and beat upon that house, and it fell not: for it was founded upon a rock" (Matt 7:25).

In spite of the threat of tornadoes, if my journey to Mullinix continues on the solid faith that Jesus holds all my moments in his hands, the possibility of reaching my destination of maximum discipleship remains secure.

For the first time in a while, I needed no medication to sleep soundly throughout the dark, stormy night.

"I'm Going to See Jesus"

Following a morning visit to the hospital, I received a call in the early evening that Paula* was not expected to live until the next day.

Rushing back to the hospital, I expected to find Paula in a comatose state or at least unable to communicate. Instead, Paula was sitting up, her back supported by two pillows as she held a phone to her left ear.

Her eyes were bright as she spoke cheerily into the phone. "Hey, Louise, I just wanted to let you know the good news." She paused to listen to the response on the other end. "No, no," she said smiling. "The doctor didn't say I'm getting better. Said there's no hope of that." Her eyes grew brighter as she exclaimed, "In fact, I'm going to see Jesus tonight!"

There must have been a stunned silence at the other end of her call because Paula said, "Did you hear me, honey? I said I'm going to see Jesus tonight!"

I could understand the shocked silence of her friend because Paula's family gathered in the hospital room also stared at their mother and grandmother, not knowing what to say. Objecting that doctors could not predict the end of life accurately or insisting "Mother, you're going to be with us a long time yet" did not seem appropriate. It would be like throwing a wet blanket over a party. Their mother was full of happy expectations. It was new to all of them.

It was also new to me, even though I had been with hundreds of families when one beloved member was approaching the end of his or her earthly walk. I've even had a few parishioners die in my arms, many of whom were at peace with their maker and approached the end with tranquility after a long life. There have been others who fought the inevitable with their last struggling breath.

In most cases the strength of the individual's faith did not appear to be the determining factor in how death was approached. More often than not, the primary variable seemed to be whether or not that particular person felt he or she had completed their reason for being. If the family of the individual was young or if the person felt there were too many tasks left unfinished, death was an unwelcome intruder. But if the person had struggled with illness and pain for a long time, death often came as a welcome relief, an angel of mercy.

*Name changed to protect privacy.

But I had never experienced anyone approaching death with Paula's exuberant expectations. After completing her phone conversation, she turned to me and said, "Pastor, did you hear the good news? I'm going to see Jesus tonight!"

Seldom have I had trouble finding the right words with as much difficulty as I did that night. I wanted to hug her and say, "Paula that's great!" But out of the corner of my eyes, I saw the family still watching in stunned silence as this scene played out before them.

Would they interpret my words of congratulations as happiness that their mother was leaving them? They obviously weren't ready for her to go. We never have enough time with those we love.

On the other hand, my primary concern as her pastor and friend was for Paula. Walking quickly to her bedside, I hugged her and said, "Sweetheart, isn't it wonderful to have a faith strong enough to give us such confident assurance of an eternal home with Jesus?"

Her enthusiasm only grew as she reached up and squeezed my neck hard. "I just can't wait, Jerry. I just can't wait!"

I stayed with Paula and her family for two or three hours until I was able to talk to her doctor in the hallway. He told me it was entirely possible that she would not survive the night, but she might also live for another day or two.

Reentering the room, I gathered everyone around the bed where we had a prayer. I can't recall the words of that prayer, but I do remember Paula's loud "Amen!" at the conclusion. Preparing to leave, I promised to be back early the next morning.

"Okay, Pastor," Paula said, more quietly now as her earlier enthusiasm had left her exhausted and her tired eyes closed.

Turning at the door, I waved back at her. Her eyes opened slightly as she said softly, "I'll tell Jesus 'hello' for you."

"You do that," I replied. "You just do that."

Early the next morning, just after sunrise, I walked into Paula's room and found her in a completely different mood. She seemed agitated and slightly depressed.

"How are you feeling today, Paula?" I asked, gently grasping her small, cool hand.

"Not too good, Pastor," she said weakly. "Didn't get to see Jesus last night." There was a hint of resentment that her body had robbed her of a wonderful homecoming.

"You know he's still waiting for you," I said. She gave me a small nod and tried to smile. She was not very successful.

Paula lived another 24 hours before she finally went to see Jesus. The frown that had appeared when her earthly journey had not ended when she expected was in the end replaced by a small, satisfied smile. I was confident Paula had reached the home she had held in her heart throughout her long life.

Living on earth while "our citizenship is in heaven" is a constant challenge (Phil 3:20). I don't even pretend to aspire to the level of success the apostle Paul reached in reconciling the two.

But I pray that whatever fears I have about death or whatever reluctance I may have about leaving this earth to claim my heavenly citizenship will be calmed and chased by memories of Paula's exuberant expectations of "going to see Jesus."

Part Six

Health Issues

The Dangers of Doctor Visits

Our younger son, Brian, came running in with face flushed and eyes wide with fear. "I just had a wreck on my bicycle and think I broke my hand!" he said excitedly.

"Yes, I think it's definitely broken," I agreed after a careful examination. "Let's put some ice on it, and we'll see the doctor in the morning."

"In the morning!" my son and wife cried in unison. "You can't be serious! The hand is broken!" But I was serious, and after a lengthy, louder-than-usual family conference, we waited until the next morning to visit the doctor.

Before you send the child welfare agency to arrest me for child neglect, let me explain.

I had broken my hand in approximately the same place playing football in high school, so I was somewhat familiar with broken hands. Coming home late from an away game with that broken hand, I let my parents continue sleeping and did not tell them about the break until the next morning.

On Friday night football game days, my very protective mother would not go to sleep until she heard me walking reasonably well on both legs. A broken hand does not interfere with one's walking if you hold it carefully, so on that evening, satisfied that I was upright and reasonably healthy, Mother had turned over and gone to sleep.

She was not happy the next morning that I had not told her about my hand, but what was the point? I knew the reaction would be far more dramatic than the break deserved.

Sure enough, upon learning about the hand, Mother was ready to cancel a planned trip that night to a Billy Graham crusade in Charlotte.

"Mother," I protested, "you and Daddy have been looking forward to that crusade for a long time, and you know George Beverly Shea will sing 'How Great Thou Art,' probably all four verses followed by the chorus after each verse. I've never known him to omit a verse or a chorus. You can't cancel your plans for a little broken hand. Besides, Coach Fortenberry is going to take me to the doctor. Go!"

After much persuasion Mother reluctantly agreed to go, and they collected a memory that lasted a lifetime. As for my hand our family doctor in Mt. Gilead said it was still too swollen for a cast and advised me to wait another day before seeing Dr. Highsmith, the only surgeon at the only county hospital, located 12 miles away in our county seat of Troy. So it was on the third day after the break that a cast was finally placed on my hand.

I have always been slow to visit doctors. In my little hometown of Mt. Gilead, we mainly went to the doctor for heart attacks and cancer and the occasional pneumonia if none of our home remedies seemed to be working.

Speaking of home remedies, my family never used this one, but the mothers of some of my friends would sometimes cut a bib out of a brown paper bag coated in homemade lard and sprinkled liberally with nutmeg. The bib was held to the chest by a tight t-shirt all night long. We could always tell when one of our class-mates was having respiratory issues by the sweet aroma of nutmeg or the occasion-al pungent odor of garlic that was substituted when one of the mothers ran out of nutmeg. Also, our sick friend would fall asleep more often than usual during class since the brown paper bib would rustle loudly all night long, making sleep difficult to come by. The number of close friends hanging out with the "patient" on any given day depended upon the particular flavor of the home remedy used the night before.

Let me clarify one thing. Over the years our family has been blessed with wonderful doctors who have also become close friends. I have much apprecia-tion for their sensitive attention and skilled care. I am neither anti-medicine nor anti-physician. Both modern medicine and good doctors are critical for our well-being, and I thank God for them.

It's just that I grew up believing the body has a remarkable ability to heal itself, so I like to at least give it a chance before calling in help too soon and often unnec-essarily. I've never rushed to visit a doctor like the rapidly growing number of folks today who seem to make an appointment at the first sniffle and even manufacture aches and pains to justify their multiple monthly doctor visits.

Besides, haven't these folks read the latest statistics? Medical errors are the third leading cause of deaths in the United States behind only heart attacks and cancer. So I guess we were on to something back in the day in my hometown.

Then, too, my perspective may have been influenced by the fact that many of my early pastors had an affinity for the Old Testament. I've sometimes wondered if maybe a somewhat obscure verse in Jeremiah stuck in my impressionable young mind at one of our second-week-in-August revivals: "Go up to Gilead. But you multiply remedies in vain; there is no healing for you" (Jer 46:11).

Well, we were right about the seriousness of heart attacks and cancer. And whether it was intuition or merely stubborn independence, we were also right about the dangers of doctor visits.

All of this causes me, once again, to reflect on the strange behavior of the human species. People who feel it is necessary to see a doctor as often as possible for their physical well-being apparently feel they can achieve spiritual health with a mere two or three visits to church per year.

Now, I must admit, there is a danger in church visits just as there is in doctor visits.

One day, I was enjoying needling a physician friend of mine with Mark's account of the woman who came to Jesus for healing: "She had suffered a great deal under the care of many doctors [for 12 years according to Mark] and had spent all she had, yet instead of getting better, she grew worse" (Mark 5:26).

Very quickly, my doctor friend replied, "Well, I have to tell you that for far longer than 12 years, I've suffered greatly at the hands of many preachers." I think he stole that line from somewhere, but I'm not sure where (just as I sometimes wonder if some of my sermon points come from a long-ago echo of other voices rather than my own original creativity).

There is that danger of suffering under many preachers. But perhaps the biggest danger in going to church is that you might experience something big and become an entirely new person. "Therefore, if anyone is in Christ, he is a new creation; the old has gone, the new has come!" (2 Cor 5:17). That kind of serious soul surgery is scary for some of us even if it means being made well.

I hope Brian will someday forgive me for delaying his visit to the doctor for a broken hand these almost 40 years ago. I was only looking out for his welfare.

And that's what I'll tell the authorities when, along the way to Mullinix—where not all my decisions lead me nearer the spiritual healing of perfect Christlikeness—they come to take me away.

Vicarious Eating

My wife looked up from where she was comfortably reclining on the couch as I walked into the den from the sun room, sniffling and wiping the last few drops of moisture from my eyes with the sleeve of my flannel shirt.

"That must have been a good movie," she said. "Watching the Hallmark Channel again?" she continued, smiling.

"No," I replied, "the Food Network."

It's been that way ever since my very conscientious physician's assistant discovered an abundance of sugar in my blood and placed me on a sugar-free, low-carb diet. Those words were hard for me to hear. In fact, they ripped a huge chunk of joy out of my life.

Being raised by a mother who was unanimously considered the "best cook in the county," I developed a keen enjoyment for the taste of food very early in life. This was back in the day before we began the awful habit of separating food into categories like "good carbs" and "bad carbs." "Bad carbs" sounds strange to me, since, to paraphrase Will Rogers, "I've never met a carbohydrate I didn't like."

The taste of good food has always been a deeply sensual experience for me, and as I grow older, sensual experiences are harder and harder to come by. I could never identify with a former parishioner who told me one day that he endured eating only to stay alive. I knew immediately that we had to search for common ground in other areas.

I have fond memories, however, on another pastoral visit, of instantaneously bonding with a woman from West Virginia when, in the middle of our getting-acquainted conversation, we slipped easily into listing our favorite childhood foods. Then, during a brief pause, she said, "Do you have time for me to whip up a quick cake of cornbread?"

I had time.

The stovetop cornbread melted the stick of butter quickly when she spread it over the entire cake while it was still in the black wrought-iron skillet. As we hungrily devoured the warm bread with a glass of cold milk, I knew food had once again forged a friendship that would last a lifetime.

So following that black Thursday when my doctor introduced me to the concept of "bad" carbohydrates, I began watching skilled chefs on the Food Network channel prepare exquisite foods for their enthusiastic guests, who exclaimed profusely about the heavenly taste while gingerly wiping the drool from the corners of their mouth.

I was not so genteel as I wiped the drool from the corners of my own mouth, vicariously experiencing each bite. I know that's a poor substitute for the real thing, but I have been a pastor for over 45 years and am something of an expert on vicarious experiences. Through the years, a sizable number of folks have afforded me an up-close look at secondhand Christianity, experienced vicariously through others who have tasted the real thing.

These are the people who, when asked if they "know the Lord," answer in the affirmative and begin reciting facts about Jesus' birth, early life, earthly ministry, crucifixion, and resurrection but never mention how he has impacted their personal lifestyle.

I have even seen them at worship services, and most have been baptized, placing their names and faces on the official pictorial directory of church membership. But their lifestyle gives no evidence that they have developed the kind of relationship with the risen Christ that transforms a follower from the inside out.

At a men's retreat some years back, I was leading a discussion concerning the sacrificial character expected of Jesus' followers. Late that evening, just before we retired for the night, one of the men came up to me and said, "Pastor, I understood what you were saying, but I never planned to get that serious about my faith." That seemed to bother him a little, but not enough to prevent his snoring loudly throughout the night in the large common room filled with bunk beds stacked side by side with soundly sleeping but far from silent men.

I appreciated his honesty, but failed to sleep as soundly as he because I knew he was voicing the experience of many who want a "plash" of religion—enough to make them appear respectable, but not enough to empower them to experience a radical change in their inner being. (By the way, I've been wanting to use that word "plash" ever since I discovered, through playing the computer game "Words" that "plash" is a "gentle splash." My sixth-grade teacher, Mrs. Roberts, told us to use a new word in a sentence as soon as possible, so I think "plash" is a good word to use for Christianity experienced vicariously.)

Of course, the family of Walnut Hills Baptist Church was mostly filled with followers feeding so eagerly on the rich food of the kingdom of heaven that their souls became too large for their bodies or even the church walls as their Christian spirit spilled over into the community and across state lines and into other countries. Those faithful folks who personally experienced the transforming power of grace kept me going as a pastor and encouraged me in my own attempts to be Christ to others.

But I have learned just enough from people who have experienced their faith secondhand to at least attempt vicarious eating when my doctor rules out my enjoying the real thing.

My sympathetic wife sits up and asks, as she hands me a tissue, "Why do you put yourself through all that?"

Taking the tissue, I reply stubbornly, "Well, it's better than nothing."

But later that night while lying in bed, restless from hunger, I wondered if it was worth it. After all, I have known firsthand the joys of the real thing, and the contrast between the authentic experience of consuming delicious food and the emptiness of secondhand eating is deeply depressing.

At least all this does remind me not to settle for substitutes on the way to Mullinix, where I am fully invaded and possessed by the Christ. Maybe that's what Paul was talking about when he wrote to the Philippians, "I consider everything a loss compared to the surpassing greatness of knowing Christ Jesus my Lord for whose sake I have lost all things. I consider them rubbish, that I may gain Christ" (Phil 3:8).

I finally fell asleep, not by counting sheep, but by counting a smorgasbord of carbohydrates leaping over a picket fence constructed of nutritionists, doctors, physician's assistants, dietitians, and other assorted food experts stacked end to end and lying one on top of the other. Poised just beyond the fence with open mouth, I snatched the carbs one by one as they cleared the fence. Oh, it was a happy night of delicious sleep, filled with voracious vicarious eating.

But when I awoke at 6:00 a.m., I was still hungry.

Bright Lights and Inside Doctors

I try to get my skin looked at once a year by a competent dermatologist since I grew up in a generation that worshiped the sun. Well, maybe we didn't worship it so much as we enjoyed feeling its warmth on our naked torsos; my brother and I took our shirts off every time we stepped outside.

My brother, Kent, is redheaded with fair skin. Consequently, in recent years, he periodically has skin cancers removed. Even though I had dark hair B.G. (before graying) and dark skin, which was a little more resistant to the sun, I feel it's prudent to have my maturing skin looked at once in a while.

It's never a pleasant experience because I don't feel I know my dermatologist well enough to strip while she examines my almost-naked body under an exceptionally bright light. I would love to have that bright light to read by, but it's far too much wattage for a full-body exam.

Although I work out three times a week and play racquetball once a week, my maturing body continues to betray me and sprouts bulges in all the wrong places. Not the kind of thing I want a member of the opposite sex, even though she is a professional, to look at too closely without strategically placed clothing.

Dermatologists do not allow enough clothing to be strategic.

It's always a relief when she finishes and leaves the room, saying, "I'll be back in a moment while you slip on your clothes." But I'm already ahead of her, lunging for my pants even before she shuts the door.

On this particular day, however, my relief was short-lived. I was halfway through buttoning my shirt when she walked back in. "Well," she said, throwing her right leg casually over the end of the exam table, "your outsides look good." I remembered how bright that light was and wondered how deeply it penetrated.

I pushed aside those disquieting thoughts as she added with a chuckle, "I've never seen a body with so many spots and blemishes with none of them looking suspicious." I tried hard to match her bright smile.

"How old are we now?" she asked, looking at me with purposeful intent.

"Well," I said, my smile growing wider as I tried hard to match her good spirits, "I'm 75, and you look to be around 43. Give me a minute." She waited, frowning impatiently while I did some figuring in my left palm with my right forefinger. "Add 75 and 43, and you get 118. Divide that by the two of us. Two into 11 is five, with one left over, bring down your eight, and divide two into 18. The way I figure it, we are 59."

My triumphant smile grew wider as hers disappeared. We just couldn't seem to get together on this smiling business. In fact, my competent dermatologist's mouth was a little pinched as she repeated, "Your outsides look good, but I'd like to talk to you about your insides." That light must have been even more powerful than I remembered.

"Hold on here," I thought to myself. "You're an outside doctor. What do you have to do with my insides?"

Her next words brought me face to face with an unpleasant revelation. "I was an internist in the beginning," she said. Just my luck to choose an outside doctor whose first go at doctoring took place on the inside. "But I never could convince people to eat the right foods, and I refused to give them pills." Pausing, she looked down at my chart. "I see you're taking pills for elevated cholesterol and high blood pressure." Leaning closer, she spat into my face, literally and figuratively, "Band-Aids! Band-Aids for conditions I know can be handled if you were more careful with your eating habits!"

In that moment I fully realized what my parishioners meant when they told me I had "quit preaching and gone to meddling." But she was on a roll now, and those rolls were mine.

"You seem to be a nice guy," she said in a tone no doubt meant to soothe my wounded ego but came across as irritatingly patronizing. Her smile was now back, but mine was gone. We just couldn't get it right.

"You seem to be a nice guy." I guess doctors, like preachers, feel a need to repeat themselves on occasion.

"You seem like a nice guy." I have always disliked repetition, especially in preachers and doctors, and wished she'd get on with her next point.

"I'd like to see you around for a few more years." Finally, something we could agree on. After all, I had just established we were only 59.

For the next few minutes, this outside doctor went on and on about what happens on my insides with plaque and blockages of arteries and other critical canals in the bodies of folks who persist in eating the "typical American diet." That sounded downright unpatriotic, and I started to tell her so, but it was getting on toward noon, and the more she talked about the foods I should avoid, the hungrier I was becoming.

Finally, she wrote down the name of a book she wanted me to read and the title of a movie I had never seen listed on Netflix. Both the book and the movie seemed to emphasize eating with a fork instead of a knife, which I guess was intended to omit those foods you have to cut, such as steak and pork chops and ribs and other wonderful red American meats.

"This will change your eating lifestyle completely," she concluded triumphantly as she handed me the paper and, of course, smiled again as if it were all such great good news.

But I was frowning again as I stuffed the slip of paper with information she considered vital into my right pants pocket. I was grateful that I had pockets again but depressed by the fact that if I kept eating the foods I enjoyed so much, we might never have an opportunity to benefit from Medicare. At 59 we had at least four more years to go.

Nodding at the receptionist on the way out, I berated myself for carelessly choosing an outside doctor who loved to mess around with my insides. I resolved then and there to exercise my freedom as an American and find a doctor who would say what I wanted to hear.

Driving back to my church study, I suddenly realized that I was having the same problem with Jesus as I did with my dermatologist. Well, actually it was James I was struggling with at the moment, whose writings, nevertheless, seemed to capture the spirit of Jesus. I was working on a series of sermons from the book written by that long-ago author, Pastor James.

Chapter after chapter, James talks about showing your faith on the outside, declaring that "faith without deeds is useless" (Jas 2:20). A good outside man. My kind of man. Faith is action that can be seen on the outside. James puts his shingle right out there: "Outside Doctor." Good deeds! Visible actions! I think I'm up to that, especially around the holidays.

Then I began wondering if I would ever catch a break when in this week's text, old Pastor James had turned out to be an internist just like my meddling dermatologist. Says I need to pay close attention to my heart or I will build blockages between myself and God, like spiritual plaque accumulating in my soul.

I just can't catch a break. Just when I thought Dr. James was going to leave my insides alone and say my outside deeds are all that matters, he throws his right leg over the corner of my desk, leans toward me, looks me straight in the eye, and keeps on pressing the point: "What causes fights and quarrels among you? Don't they come from your desires that battle within you?" (Jas 4:1).

Just can't seem to catch a break. Neither my dermatologist nor James will leave my insides alone. Of course, I don't want blockages in my arteries or my soul to cut short my earthly journey or my spiritual journey to Mullinix.

But I still have trouble smiling about it.

Part Seven

Passing Thoughts

How I Got Jimmy Carter Elected President

Political campaigns, especially presidential contests, leave me exhausted and highly agitated. Seeking escape, I find myself watching more and more of the National Geographic Wild channel, preferring natural ferocious animal behavior in the wild to the contrived animal behavior of national politics.

By the way, on a recent segment, I heard an ornithologist say, "Flashy feathers and showmanship always win the day for the males to attract females." I've noticed that in most things we have failed to move beyond such birdbrain behavior, as "flashy feathers and showmanship" still seem to attract the most attention.

But the other day in a weak moment, my mind wandered back to a time when I was drawn into the center ring of the political circus and succeeded in getting Jimmy Carter elected president. That doesn't sound very modest for a retired pastor who has spent most of his life trying hard to be humble. But facts are facts. History is history—until, of course, someone tries to rewrite it.

This is not a rewrite. This is an account of exactly how it happened. I simply felt it was time to set the record straight, even if it means correcting all the history books.

On October 22, 1976, Jimmy Carter and Gerald Ford came to Williamsburg, Virginia, for the last of their debates during the presidential campaign of that historic year in our nation's history. The debate took place in Phi Beta Kappa Hall on the campus of the College of William and Mary, located a half mile down Jamestown Road from our church, Walnut Hills Baptist.

Following the debate, the two candidates moved over to what was then William and Mary Hall, now Kaplan Arena, for a brief appearance and short speech.

That was the place and time I got Jimmy Carter elected president.

My sister-in-law, Angela, better known as "Lulu," was living with our family at the time and persuaded me to accompany her to the events at W&M Hall. I was reluctant because I had already decided on my vote and was fearful one of the candidates would change his mind on an issue (this was back in the good ol' days when politicians still talked about things with real substance) and I would have to decide on my vote all over again.

But I went. Besides, my step was there. And that step is what this story is all about.

As we walked into W&M Hall, a mass of people filled every seat, and many more were standing. I grabbed Lulu's arm and turned to leave when Lester Hooker Jr., a good friend and church member who sat on the back pew every Sunday morning, called out, "Jerry, I've got a couple seats down front that I'm not going to use." Lester was the first director of W&M Hall and provided us with some excellent seats for basketball games. But that's another story.

Asking us to follow, Lester ushered us into a roped-off area with two empty seats in the fourth row from the stage. I wasn't eager to be that close to the cameras representing all the major networks since I hadn't shaved my five o'clock shadow or bothered to put on a tie. Now you young folks need to understand that this was back in the day when wearing a tie was a sure sign of respectability and a scruffy face was highly suspect.

But at least down here near the front I was closer to my step, so I decided to risk my reputation of being a clean-cut pastor.

Earlier in the week, as he was making preparations for the appearance of the presidential candidates, Lester called and asked if he could borrow my step. The step to which he was referring was well-known around the church. It was about six inches high and covered with a leftover scrap of the green carpet we had used for the center aisle in our first little sanctuary.

I was about 5'8" B.S. (before shrinkage) in my Sunday shoes, and being inexperienced in such things, our church had purchased a pulpit that measured exactly 5'8" at its highest point. John Owens, one of our loyal members, a one-man lockup committee, felt my preaching might be more effective if folks could actually see my face, so he built a step on which I could stand throughout thousands of sermons and make eye contact without standing on my tiptoes.

That was the step Lester had asked to borrow.

Seems that Jimmy Carter's people wanted him to look as tall as Gerald Ford for the television cameras. As you know, elections are often determined by such shallow, superficial perceptions. History has shown that the external appearance of a candidate is far more important than internal considerations like character or convictions or values. Clearly aware of what happened to Nixon and the notorious dark circles under his eyes, which didn't fare well against Kennedy's smooth face and good looks, Carter's people did not want him to lose the election simply because he was shorter than Gerald Ford.

Thus, it became more and more obvious that the outcome of the election rested on the power of my step.

President Ford spoke first, and as he walked off stage right, Lester immediately came walking out from stage left with the step, placing it carefully in front of the podium. I leaped up from my seat and began applauding wildly. The woman to my right, whom I had spoken to briefly as I had taken my seat earlier, jumped up beside me, crying out, "Where is he? Where is he?"

"No, no," I said, "that's my step!"

The woman quickly sank back, almost sitting in her boyfriend's lap, putting as much distance between us as possible.

About that time Jimmy Carter walked out confidently but hesitated as he looked down at my step covered with sanctuary carpet and built sturdy enough to last for thousands of sermons delivered with sincere eye contact. Panic gripped me as I feared he was going to shove my step aside and with that simple movement remove forever and ever my place in history. But finally, with a resigned shake of his head, Jimmy Carter lifted his right leg and then his left and took his place on my step.

With a huge sigh of relief, I settled back and was pleased to see that, yes, Jimmy Carter was exactly one inch taller than Gerald Ford. I knew in that moment that Carter had won the election, so the counting of votes a couple weeks later was, for me, extremely anticlimactic.

After his speech, soon-to-be-president Carter began shaking hands with folks across the ropes. As my turn came, I shook his hand vigorously and said with unbridled pride, "That was my step that made you taller than President Ford." Carter responded with a puzzled look, so I assumed he was too filled with gratitude to reply.

Seeing that I had just spoken to candidate Carter, a reporter from CBS shoved a microphone in front of my face and asked, "Could I ask you a question?"

"Well," I replied, "I didn't shave and forgot my tie, but I guess it'll be all right."

Leaning in closer, the reporter asked, "What did you think of Mr. Carter's speech?"

"Well," I responded with what I intended to be a warm smile, but I must have failed because a friend in Kentucky watching the telecast called later that night and said it looked a lot like a smirk. "I really liked his platform."

"Could you expound on that a little bit?" the reporter asked.

With my smile growing wider until I figured it rivaled Sheriff Andy's of Mayberry fame, I replied, "John Owens built it."

Well, that's how I got Jimmy Carter elected president. If any fact-checkers want to investigate the veracity of my story, come examine the picture hanging on my study wall of Carter standing on my step and smiling at the cameras.

I'm deeply grateful to Chip Delano for taking that picture. Chip, a William and Mary student and member of Walnut Hills at the time, was also an avid photographer. Being quite familiar with my step, he told me recently how he was careful to position himself to the side of the podium so he could include my step in his picture of Carter on that historic evening. Chip is now a lawyer in Richmond, Virginia, and would make an excellent witness to the authenticity of this account.

Four years later, after President Carter's defeat in the next election to Reagan, I sent him the picture Chip had taken with an explanation of the events of that day in Williamsburg. I was deeply grateful that he was kind enough to autograph the picture and send it back. I had kind of hoped he would say something like "Thanks for the lift" or "I could never have risen that high without you." But I was happy to settle for the autograph.

I also told him I had voted for him, not because he used my step, but because he almost did not use the step. I was close enough to see his displeasure at having to step on that little height extender and that he only did so reluctantly. In that moment I felt I had seen something of his character, one that was impatient with superficial, external appearances.

Being a student of the Bible and a Sunday school teacher, President Carter had no doubt come across Jesus' words to the teachers of the law and Pharisees: "You hypocrites!… First clean the inside of the dish and then the outside also will be clean" (Matt 23:25–26). These words have helped me on my journey toward Mullinix, that place of full Christlikeness, as I have tried hard to distinguish between the true and the false by looking beneath outer appearances and discovering the inner health at the core of the individual.

By the way, I would like the fact-checkers to call me for an appointment before they show up at my front door. Apparently, our culture has fallen hook, line, and sinker for the claim of a commercial I heard recently. The ad was promising quick hair growth: "Don't forget," the paid actor with a head full of thick, wavy black hair said solemnly, "in our culture, appearance is everything!"

So call me before the fact-checkers show up. I want to shave and put on a nice Carolina blue tie for those majority of folks who still measure value and ability by "flashy feathers and showmanship."

Don't Judge My Fear of Flying

I told my wife when I retired from Walnut Hills Baptist Church in Williamsburg, Virginia, after 35 years as pastor, that I was also retiring from flying.

The church had generously sent us on many wonderful trips that required planes to reach our destination during our time there. So I said my prayers, took my tranquilizers, and climbed on board. Parishioners gave me a hard time, saying a man of faith should feel comfortable being that much closer to heaven.

"One big problem," I protested. "Don't you realize that you have to come crashing down before you can go back up? It's the coming down that bothers me, not the going up."

The closest I came to feeling comfortable on a plane was when we flew to the Holy Land in 1996 on one of those huge two-story planes/hotels belonging to the Israeli national airline, El Al—a tremendous gift from the church on the occasion of our 30th anniversary of serving Walnut Hills.

The plane was so huge that it was impossible to feel claustrophobic with so much room to roam, even climbing a flight of stairs to the upper level of seats. But I made a mistake in picking up a brochure as I took my seat halfway down the wide aisle. The brochure extolled the virtues of the airline and made this bold statement: "This airline has the best crash record in the world."

Wait a minute! Is there such a thing as a good crash record? Talk about oxymorons! "So much for feeling good about flying," I muttered as I popped another tranquilizer.

But I resigned myself to the 10-plus-hour flight from New York to Tel Aviv, Israel, because I was determined to "walk where Jesus walked." If I died, I figured I would at least be moving in the right direction.

I think my fear of flying, in part at least, dates back to the early 1970s when a member of our church bought a little two-seater plane and invited me to join him on a "fun short flight." Sacrifices are often needed to keep parishioners happy.

My pilot friend was a big man, and when he got in first, I wondered where I was supposed to sit. He was taking up all of his seat and half of mine. "Climb in," he said with a wide grin, stirring up a childhood memory of the spider's invitation to the fly.

Making myself as small as possible, I struggled into what he laughingly called "the co-pilot's seat." I strained to return his smile, realizing that if he had a heart attack, I was the pilot. I had struggled all through elementary school to keep those little notebook paper airplanes from propelling straight to the ground. What chance did I have with a real airplane?

With my arms pinned to my sides after my friend had reached over with his huge hand and slammed the cockpit door shut, we took off from the little Jamestown airport into a wind my pilot laughingly described as "just within the safe limits" for planes of this size.

Why did he have to laugh when he said things like that?

But we were in the air now, bouncing and swerving at the mercy of every little air current passing by. Big as my friend was, I couldn't understand why Jeff wasn't more of a stabilizing force.

"Let's go check out the church," he said cheerfully. I've been with a number of people who journeyed toward death quite cheerfully, and I admired their faith. But never before had anyone been taking me with them. It gave a little different perspective to the experience of pleasant passing.

Jeff had wanted to go see the church because a tree had fallen on the roof, opening a big hole just above the pulpit. To tell the truth, since I have always been an outdoors person, it was not an unpleasant experience preaching inside while looking straight into the heavens. But looking at that hole from above rather than from below was definitely unpleasant.

"There it is!" Jeff called out, still as happy as a bird in flight. "Can you see the blue tarp over the hole?"

"Y-y-yes," I stammered in a voice bearing no resemblance at all to my best pulpit voice.

"Let me give you a better look," Jeff called out and turned the little model airplane on its side so that I dangled above the damaged roof, which was growing closer and closer.

"I see it! I see it!" I cried in a voice that I was sure exposed the panic I was vainly trying to hide.

Still laughing, Jeff brought the plane level so we could continue bouncing along approximately parallel to Mother Earth, whom I desperately wished would immediately cradle me safely in her mother's arms. Actually, at that moment, any mother's arms would have been acceptable.

After about 30 more minutes of aimless flight, I realized, with much relief, that we were finally circling back toward Jamestown airport. I entertained the wild hope that I might live to preach another day. That hope was immediately crushed as we swooped in for a landing, only to rise, bouncing back into the low-hanging clouds with a deep roar.

"Coming in a little too fast," Jeff chuckled as he goosed the plane into full throttle. Secretly, I think he had looked over at my face and was not satisfied with that particular shade of green and thought he would try for a richer color.

Whatever his intention, Jeff succeeded as he made another aborted swoop toward the landing strip while saying, "Let's try it one more time," sounding much like one of my children wanting to play with his favorite toy just a few more minutes.

Thankfully, we landed on the third try, and I hastily unfastened my seat belt, opened the door, and tumbled to the ground. Jeff was busily shutting everything down and didn't notice how enthusiastically I was embracing and kissing the ground, reluctant to rise and test my trembling legs.

I hope this story will stop, or at least slow you, in being so judgmental in calling my fear of flying a "lack of faith." Perhaps it will even plant a seed of understanding in your heart.

I have a history.

All of us do, of course—a past that influences and sometimes controls our present. But surely the one who "has overcome the world" (John 16:33) can help all us wounded folks overcome our past.

All this does remind me, however, that while going to Mullinix, that place where I am empowered to reflect more accurately the true nature of our Lord, I need to be slow to judge and quick to offer grace to those I meet along the way.

I don't know their history.

This might be a good place for a word of wisdom from the apostle Paul: "You, therefore, have no excuse, you who pass judgment on someone else, for at whatever point you are judging the other, you are condemning yourself, because you who pass judgment are doing the same things" (Rom 2:1).

I don't think he was talking about fear of flying, but he easily could have been.

Too Small?

I shouldn't have been surprised when I saw on the sports page some time back that a professional woman golfer asked for another caddy because the one assigned to her was too short.

It was of no consequence to her that the local college student assigned to carry her bags was strong and capable and spent hours preparing to be the best caddy he could be, even arriving 90 minutes early for the 8:00 a.m. Monday start. None of that mattered to the professional golfer. She took one look at his diminutive size and said, "Do you have anyone bigger?"

I repeat. I shouldn't have been surprised since sports, like the rest of the world of entertainment, tends to mirror society rather than transform it. And personal observation, along with serious studies, have shown that our society has a prejudicial preference for prodigiousness.

In fact, I came across an article in the newspaper citing a University of Florida study saying that tall people actually earn more money for the same work than short people. To those women who thought such pay discrimination only happened to them, say "hello" to a large company of short-changed short people.

After reading that tall people make more money for the same amount of work than short people, a short colleague of mine started wearing cowboy boots with five-inch heels. A few weeks after beginning that practice, however, he was very discouraged. The budget committee hadn't even noticed his increased height, so his salary had not increased.

Initially, I took that as a hopeful sign. "Maybe," I thought, "since my friend's increased inches were not reflected in his salary, maybe churches don't mirror larger society as much as it sometimes appears."

I really got excited about that possibility. Since my friend's increased height failed to result in an increase in remuneration, maybe the church was listening to Jesus instead of society and was looking for other criteria as being worthy of its financial blessings. I held tightly to that exciting possibility for several weeks, until I attended a pastors' conference, which is a wonderful place to have your illusions burst.

Standing in line to receive our light lunch, I overheard two colleagues talking. By the way, it's always a "light" lunch at gatherings of overweight ministers. "For your own good," our hostess explained. One week, we had a famed gospel singer perform. As he sat down at the piano, his first words were, "I'll do the best I can. But I don't have much energy after that puny meal." Well, he was a big man with an appetite to match his girth, and I've heard that celebrities do like to request special foods in order to perform their best. This man was no different. I wish he had been. His poor spirit drowned out most of his upbeat gospel music.

But back to the bursting of my latest illusion. Standing in the food line, I overheard the two men in front of me discussing the latest pastoral addition to our association.

"Have you had a chance to meet the new pastor down the street?" one asked.

The man standing in front of him replied, "Just briefly."

"What's he like?"

"Oh, he's a great big tall fellow." This vital information was offered with a wide, pleased smile.

I continued listening, hoping for a little more in-depth description of our new colleague, but it never came.

"How tall would you say he is?" the first man continued.

"At least 6'6"."

"Really? That tall?"

"Probably more," his companion replied, quite satisfied with his description.

"Bet folks will pay attention to him," the second man replied. They both were shaking their heads in wonder as they reached for their light lunch, which seemed to disappoint them. Apparently, size mattered on their plates as well as in the pulpit.

Later that same week, I bumped into a friend with whom I had served on several associational committees and whose sense of discernment I had come to admire. I also knew he was a member of the church that had welcomed the new pastor.

I said cheerfully, "I hear you have a new pastor."

"Yes," he replied, his eyes twinkling.

"What's he like?"

"Oh, he's a great big tall fellow."

I nodded, trying hard to return his smile, and quickly walked away.

During the night of that same day, I had one of those dreams that usually occur after I've eaten too much spicy Mexican food. Ghostlike visitors walked into my bedroom with exciting news. Seems they had experienced the unique privilege of visiting heaven and hell and were ready to provide answers that I could pass on to my inquisitive parishioners. This was good stuff.

Their glowing report of heaven filled me with excitement and yearning, and I was eager to relay their descriptions in my next sermon.

But when they started describing hell, I broke out in a cold sweat. It was awful. I had always been skeptical of his methods, but now I wondered if maybe Jonathan Edwards had it right when he would dangle his parishioners over the flaming pits of hell, leaving them trembling in fear.

"But tell me," I finally stammered. "If hell is that terrible, what's the devil like?"

"Oh," they said, shaking their heads in wonder, "he's a great big tall fellow."

Along the way to Mullinix, I try hard to remember God's words to Samuel: "Do not consider his appearance or his height, for I have rejected him. The LORD does not look at the things man looks at. Man looks at the outward appearance, but the LORD looks at the heart" (1 Sam 16:7).

The other day, I ran into my friend and asked how his new pastor was doing. With a sad face he said, "He barely lasted a year. He was such a poor pastor, didn't seem to care much about any of us. Probably should have lasted no more than six months."

Pausing briefly, he continued, "But he was so tall we hated to ask him to leave."

At a Bar in Key West

With a delicious-smelling tuna wrap in one hand and a large frosty bottle of water in the other, I turned from the bar to search for my wife and share this small meal with her. One high step led from the outdoor bar/grill, and then a harder-to-see smaller step deposited guests onto the wooden boardwalk running along the white sand beach. I had no problem with the high step. The small step was the one I didn't see, and I landed with a resounding belly flop, rattling two loose boards on the ancient boardwalk.

When I retired after 35 years as pastor of Walnut Hills Baptist Church in Williamsburg, Virginia, I also retired from flying. I determined that, given my strong dislike of flying, I had seen all I needed to see except those wonders I could reach by car or train.

So when a young woman who had grown up in our church asked me to officiate at her wedding in an exotic setting, I told her I would be delighted to, if that exotic setting was in the lower 48, which I could reach without leaving the ground. She was not particularly happy with those boundaries but finally decided she could be satisfied with the botanical gardens at the very southern tip of Key West, Florida, 30-some miles from Cuba.

It was a delightful experience being a tourist in an intriguing place. I even bought an Ernest Hemingway t-shirt, which I still wear each time I sit down to write the next great American novel.

We spent the first two nights in a nearby hotel, courtesy of the bride and groom. Following the wedding, however, we moved to the Key West Hyatt Resort with the help of a relative employed by the Hyatt organization.

Unfortunately, the move from the hotel to the resort coincided with a University of North Carolina Tar Heels basketball game. I was a junior at Chapel Hill when the legendary Dean Smith became head coach, so I love the Tar Heels far more than a good Christian should.

When we arrived at the resort at noon, we discovered that our suite was not going to be ready for another couple hours. Panic time! The game began at noon.

That's how I found myself at a lovely bar/grill on a boardwalk next to the beautiful, multihued blue waters of the Gulf of Mexico. I told the petite blonde girl behind the bar of my desperate situation and how the desk clerk inside quickly tired of seeing a grown man cry and sent me back here to possibly watch the game on the bar television.

It could only be described as a miracle that the bartender had a younger brother who was entering Chapel Hill that fall, so she fully understood my sickness. Not only did she angle the large-screen television in my direction as I sat at the bar, but she kept refilling my water glass along with the dish of fancy nuts she had placed in front of me.

"You're in luck," she said with a smile revealing gleaming white teeth. "We don't usually have expensive nuts like these," she said warmly.

"I can understand that," I replied appreciatively. "Our family can't afford nuts like these except at Christmas." My hostess's devoted attentiveness to my needs during the next two hours may have been the greatest benefit I had received thus far from a degree at the University of North Carolina.

At halftime Carolina was comfortably ahead, so I tore my attention away from the game and ordered a tuna salad wrap and a bottle of water to share with my wife, who was lounging by the nearby swimming pool. With my head up and eyes searching for my wife, that small step was tragically easy to miss.

I landed with such a loud belly flop that, out of the corner of my eye, I was sure I saw the two ships heading out in the gulf make a slow right turn to check it out.

My knees hurt terribly, but even worse was the pain to my pride inflicted by all those curious faces suddenly appearing at every resort window. The swimming pool loungers were also hanging over the railing around the pool in search of the source of the loud explosion.

I looked up as I lay supine on the splintery boardwalk and saw a frowning young mother shielding her two small children from the disastrous scene a few feet away. Her thoughts were easy to read: "Unbelievable! A man his age staggering out of a bar at 1:30 in the afternoon! And at such a nice place as this!"

I wanted to run after her and explain that it was an open-air bar/grill and I was using the grill part, not the bar part, while drinking water and eating fancy nuts that we could only afford at Christmas and how I had spent my whole life trying not to "cause one of these little ones to stumble" (Luke 17:2).

But my knees hurt too severely to run. I painfully bent over to pick up the mess my tuna wrap had made on the boardwalk. With relief I saw a pair of familiar hands reaching out to help me regain my equilibrium. I was a little hurt, however, when I saw that my wife had carefully draped a large beach towel around her head in an effort to hide her face.

We took the spoiled tuna wrap back to the open-air bar/grill and dumped it in the trash barrel near that little step I had failed to negotiate. My young friend behind the bar looked at me with a furrow of concern on her brow.

"Honey," she said, "are you all right?" Then she placed her cool, slender right hand gently on the aching left wrist I had used in breaking my fall. That helped. "Here," she added, sliding the dish closer, "have some more nuts." And I did, because Christmas was still several months away.

Sometimes on the way to Mullinix, that place where Christ is fully formed in me, I fall flat on my face, and people misunderstand my motives, judging unfairly and making it difficult for me to pick myself up and begin again.

But the hopeful word is that our failures and troubles can actually enhance the journey: "We also rejoice in our sufferings, because we know that suffering produces perseverance; perseverance, character; and character, hope" (Rom 5:3–4).

I've learned to cling to those words—especially when I do a full-out belly flop on a public boardwalk. I've also learned to look out for those vicious little steps along the way. The little steps are the hardest to see and often the trickiest to negotiate.

Good Stories Never Grow Old

Over the years my friends and parishioners have learned to introduce all their stories with the disclaimer, "Jerry, you've probably heard this one, but…" Unfortunately, 99 times out of 100, I have heard it. But if they are terribly excited about sharing a "new" story, good manners require that I deny ever hearing it and laugh along with them.

Besides, a really good story never gets old and often improves with age. I told my father one day that his stories seemed to get longer each year. Smiling wryly, he replied, "Well, Son, it's like this. The older I get, the more details I seem to remember."

Three men have contributed most to my love for and my crowded memory bank of stories: my father; my maternal grandfather, Pa-Pa; and my Uncle G. A., Mother's only brother. They were all gifted storytellers, and the vividness of the details included in their stories have been embedded in my memory for life.

Good stories possess enduring power, and most of the stories I heard growing up came by oral tradition, passed down from generation to generation. Now, after hearing stories for over 75 years and using most of them as illustrations in thousands of sermons and lessons and lectures, it's a cause for celebration when I get a whiff of newness in any story. But as I said, my enjoyment of a story doesn't rest on newness. The way it is told is the most critical variable in bringing out the richness of any story.

So hearing stories unfold in a unique manner was one of my motivations when making a trip home to stop by and visit Uncle G. A. By this time, he was the only one left of the three storytellers who enthralled me throughout their lives.

In his later years I would find G. A. sitting under the open back stoop beside the well that in an earlier time provided water for my mother's family. As a young boy I was intrigued by the bucket rope winding and unwinding around the smooth, rounded log turned by an iron handle worn smooth with use. Watching in fascination as the bucket plummeted down the open shaft, I listened for the satisfying splash as it crashed into the cool, refreshing water I would soon be drinking from a tin dipper hanging from a nail driven into the wooden frame of the well.

The well opening was now sealed over with a concrete slab beside which G. A. placed his lawn chair and watched the cars go by. On my visits I would grab another lawn chair and sit facing him, ready for the retelling of stories that strengthened the bonds between past and present. Sometimes, G. A's wife, Helen, joined us, adding an interesting dimension to the storytelling.

From time to time, G. A. would look over at his wife in the middle of a story and ask, "Helen, how many young'uns did Reid have? Yeah, that's right. Five. Two girls and three boys. You 'member their names?"

Without waiting for an answer, he continued, "Youngest had a little facial tic, didn' he? Seem to 'member his mama said the tic came from flinching from his daddy's slaps, most which never landed." G. A. paused just long enough to slap his leg and punctuate his story with a short, explosive laugh.

"Near as I c'n recall, the tic was on the boy's left side, and his daddy was right-handed, so I guess that's right." Nodding his head, satisfied that his deductions were correct, G. A. said, "Ol' Man Reid Sedberry's aim never was much 'count." He looked up at a low-hanging cloud passing by, his mind reaching back to another time.

"I 'member the time a bunch of us went squirrel hunting with the little fice we used to have" (some folks say the proper name for that breed is "feist," but in the Piedmont region of North Carolina, we called them "fice" dogs).

"You 'member 'im, don't you, Jerry?"

"Reid Sedberry?" I asked.

"No," G. A. guffawed again. "The little fice. White with small black spots on his sides and legs. Called 'im Max. Pretty as a speckled pup in a red wagon pulled by a lil' blue-eyed girl in a yella dress." Jerking himself back to the present, G. A. continued, "Good squirrel dog, too."

Not sure that I remembered Max, but not wanting to interrupt the story, I nodded, and G. A. continued. "Well, Max'd treed this squirrel up a big hickory tree, and that rascal laid down on a limb with just the top part of 'is back showing. Ol' Man Sedberry wanted the shot with his ol' beat-up .22 rifle he got from his wife on their first anniversary. Least, I think it was the first."

Turning toward his wife again, he said, "Helen, was it 'is first anniversary or mebbe his second. Been many years ago, so I ain't sure about that." G. A. was silent for a moment, worried he wasn't getting the details exactly right.

"Anyway, we gave 'im the shot, and Ol' Man Sedberry hit a little limb with about two dozen hickory nuts on it. Landed right on top of us, but out of the corner of my eye, I saw that squirrel jump onto the limb of a big oak tree, and then I lost sight of 'im altogether."

G. A. slapped his leg again and, with a reddened face, let out his usual short but loud burst of laughter, which resounded throughout the yard and across the black asphalt road to the store that still held the sign "Haywood's Grocery" even though it was now used only for storage.

"Naw, Ol' Man Sedberry never did have much of a aim. So I don't think his boy with th' facial tic felt too many of those slaps."

In telling and retelling his stories, Uncle G. A. always wandered into seemingly insignificant details that added very little additional information but provided a lot of color and enjoyment for both of us. Besides, he always found his way back and eventually completed the story.

The frequency of my trips to North Carolina has diminished since G. A. has now joined the list of storytellers who have been silenced by death. Only Helen remains in the old farmhouse still permeated with the aroma of family roots, like the old coats and other assorted heavy outerwear that had hung in a back hall during my boyhood.

G. A. finally succumbed to the heart disease he fought for many years. I think I know at least part of the reason for his heart troubles—goat milk.

My uncle taught me many things, but he never was able to instill in me his love for goat milk. I remember watching him drink it warm from the milk bucket and then smack his lips on the way to the kitchen, where the raw, creamy milk would be strained through cheesecloth into a gallon Mason jug. The straining was needed to remove all the specks and bits of straw his restless nanny goat had kicked into the white milk pail during the milking.

Maybe it was good that I resisted G. A.'s invitation to "taste it, Son. It's better than cow milk." Although goat milk has about the same fat content as milk from a cow, a number of modern studies say goat milk is superior in nutrients, easier to digest, and tastes better.

However, I think that "tastes better" part may have been G. A.'s downfall. He couldn't get enough of that white liquid, so he owned a succession of nanny goats through the years, all of whom proved to be quite productive. If I had not resisted his invitation to "try it," I may have succumbed to G. A.'s lifetime struggle with a goat milk drinking addiction. I understand that drinking problems are often genetic in nature.

So I have a suspicion that it was, at least in part, G. A.'s lack of moderation in drinking goat milk that contributed to the clogging of his arteries. In an effort to combat the clogging, besides numerous surgeries, his doctor had put him on a diet of 1,000 calories a day, almost bringing G. A. to tears as he told me during one of my visits, "Son, I'm so weak on 1,000 calories a day that I cain't even milk a goat."

Maybe being unable to milk a goat was a part of the doctor's plan for G. A. all along.

I've noticed that in my journeying toward Mullinix, I exhibit some of the same tendencies found in G. A.'s storytelling. Some days, I wander down circuitous paths that add nothing at all to my progress toward being fully possessed by the Christ.

Those side roads, however, are often where I meet the most colorful people and the most curious critters—people and critters who give me hints and nudges, reminding me of what I need to do to get back to the most direct route toward my destination.

Gulping another deep drink of God's infinite grace, I renew my journey, eternally grateful that God has a passion for making me the person I was created to be.

Now that's an old story itself, made new with each retelling.

Epilogue: Coming Home

A friend of mine over in Deltaville, Virginia, called one day while I was working on a sermon during my tenure as interim pastor of Zoar Baptist Church. Eddie Harrow shares my love of stories, and he had just thought of one he knew I would appreciate. I think a lawyer friend of his had told this story a few years earlier.

The way I remember it, a young man was plowing behind a pair of black mules when his chronic restlessness got the best of him. Stopping in the middle of a row, he draped the lines over the plow handles, turned his back on the mules still harnessed to the plow, and disappeared down the road.

Two years later, the young man's father was plowing in that same field when he looked up to see his son walking unsteadily down the road with torn denim shirt, worn jeans, a faded railroad cap on his head, and a face deeply furrowed with many more worry lines than he had when he left.

Calling out a loud "Whoa!" to his team of mules, the father walked across the corn field to meet his son. "Boy," he said, so relieved to see his son that his anger over the son's sudden departure disappeared completely. "Boy," he repeated, "how in the world did you get so beat down?"

Lifting his weary head and staring blankly at his father, the young man answered simply, "Coming home."

"Coming home," which I have called "Mullinix," is not an easy journey. Living as citizens of heaven (our ultimate home) while at the same time being citizens of this world is not a simple thing. The coming of God's kingdom in me "as it is in heaven" is a lifelong journey.

When the trip has become particularly difficult and I have been tempted to give the whole thing up as impossible for mere humans, a restless emptiness (which feels a lot like "homesickness") has set me on my way again. Perhaps that's the human condition Augustine of Hippo was addressing in his Confessions: "Thou hast made us for thyself, O Lord, and our heart is restless until it finds its rest in Thee."

On occasion I would hear Pa-Pa add an apostrophe "s" to his customary greeting, "going to Mullinix," making it the possessive, "going to Mullinix's." Maybe the possessive case of the word "Mullinix" is the correct designation after all. Mullinix is not so much something to be found and possessed as it is that place where I am possessed by one outside myself.

Therefore, "home," or "Mullinix," that place where I fully "rest" in God, is not something to be achieved by my own efforts but by allowing the risen Christ to love me unconditionally. If I am constantly seeking to prove my worth by reaching a higher plane of spirituality as a follower of Jesus, I am always vulnerable to discouragement and failure. But when I remind myself that his love is unconditional and his grace is unlimited, the constant voice of self-condemnation and hopelessness is silenced. My biggest job, then, is to learn to live as one who is loved beyond all reason.

So I'm still "going to Mullinix." But somewhere along the way, I began trusting Jesus Christ to do the heavy lifting while my task became submitting to being lifted. Maybe that was something of what Paul experienced: "When I am weak, then I am strong" (2 Cor 12:10).

My desire for reaching home has not waned with the passing years. The nudges and hints along the way still come from people and critters and events. But now I see a little more clearly, through all of them, the magnetic power of the infinite love of a Father-God waiting for his wandering son to make his weary way home: "While he was still a long way off, his father saw him and was filled with compassion for him" (Luke 15:20b).

"Son, how did you get so beat up?"

"Coming home."

On my best days I can feel home just ahead, beyond the crest of the next hill, where it sounds like they're getting ready for a party.

CPSIA information can be obtained
at www.ICGtesting.com
Printed in the USA
FSHW01n1502250418
47277FS

9 781635 280302